More
Creative Craft
Activities

Edited by Caroline Clark Myers

Foreword

Craft activities have been found to be helpful in gaining children's attention and stimulating their imagination. Creative projects which are seasonal or are related to specific holidays may supplement schoolwork. The activities in this Handbook have been selected from varied materials published in HIGHLIGHTS FOR CHILDREN. The directions are clear and easy to follow. The Handbook offers many opportunities to the child for creative expression. The materials are inexpensive or free and readily available. *More Creative Craft Activities* provides children additional projects of the type found in the earlier Handbook, *Creative Craft Activities*.

— *The Editors*, HIGHLIGHTS FOR CHILDREN

Myers, Caroline Elizabeth (Clark), comp.
  More creative craft activities.

  (Highlights jumbo handbooks)
  SUMMARY: More than 300 craft ideas for seasonal, holiday, and year-round projects using materials readily available in the home or classroom.
  "Selected from varied materials published in Highlights for children."
  1. Handicraft—Juvenile literature.
1. Handicraft I. Highlights for children.
II. Title.
TT160.M93   745.5'05   73-8898
ISBN 0-87534-556-5

Airy Decorations

By Evelyn Minshull

Both breezy and easy are these Halloween creatures. They may be used either as large party favors set atop a paper cup, or as party decorations. If you want to hang them from the ceiling, keep the tied end of the balloon topside. If they're for the younger set who might like to tow them through the air, keep the tied end at the bottom and attach a long string. However you use them, they are bright and fun. Here is how they are made.

Blow up round balloons. Tie securely. Decorate.

Pumpkin

Draw lines from top to bottom to represent the sections of the pumpkin. Cut features from black construction paper and tape in place with small strips of transparent cellophane tape. Twist a green pipe cleaner for the stem. Cut a leaf or two from dark-green construction paper. Draw on veins. Attach to the stem.

Witch

From a 9-inch square of black construction paper, cut on the curved line as shown. Roll into a witch's hat and tape down the seam. Fringe the long side for the hair. Tape the hat in place. Draw more hair and the witch's features.

Owl

Cut the large V-shape from black construction paper, the pupils of the eyes from green paper, and the bill from orange paper. Draw on the other lines and tape the features in place.

Cat

Draw the outlines for the slanted eyes, the mouth, and the dots at the base of the whiskers. Whiskers are narrow strips of paper. Cut ears from paper, slit up the center, and fold one side under the other. Tape in place. The centers of the eyes and the nose may be drawn, or cut from paper and taped on.

Remember, please, that balloons are fragile. Even with care, an occasional one may explode as you work on it and give YOU a Halloween scare!

3

Pumpkin Rocks

By Lee Lindeman

Paint a nice, smooth, pumpkin-shaped rock the color of a pumpkin. Use tempera, poster, or acrylic paint. Let the pumpkin rock dry.

Add details with tempera, dry marker, or crayon. Cut a stem and leaf from green felt and glue onto the pumpkin.

Pumpkin rocks can be used as paperweights or as decorations on a shelf or table.

Salt-spout Owl

By Agnes Choate Wonson

Draw an owl on cardboard and color it. Paper reinforcement rings may be used for the whites of the eyes. Use the tin spout from a salt box for the bill, inserting the sides through slits in the card. Fasten a piece of cellophane tape from the card to the top of the spout so the bill may open and close.

Large Mosaic Picture

By Helen A. Thomas

Find several pieces of paper that vary in color as well as texture. Cut these into small pieces. With a dark crayon divide a sheet of paper about 12 by 18 inches into sections by using four lines. In each section glue pieces of the same color. Use a different color in each section. Put a border around the edge with crayon.

Jack-o'-lantern Totem Pole   By Sylvia Sanders

This is a good project for a family or other group when everyone wants to make his own jack-o'-lantern. Select the pumpkins carefully so they will fit together well. You will need a big one for the bottom, then smaller and smaller ones. Each one should have a nice flat bottom so your totem pole will stand straight.

Starting with the bottom pumpkin, cut a fairly large hole in the top and set the next-sized pumpkin in the opening. Continue this on up the totem pole. The top of only the top pumpkin need be saved.

Scrape out the insides and cut a different face into each pumpkin. Be sure the mouth isn't too near the bottom or the eyes too near the top.

Outline the eyes, nose, and mouth with felt pens. You may also want to add eyebrows, eyelashes, dimples, wrinkles, moustaches, and white poster-paint teeth. A carrot stuck through a round nose, or two carrots used as horns for the top pumpkin will add a different note.

You can light your jack-o'-lanterns by placing a small flashlight in each or with a string of Christmas lights. Cut small notches in the top of each pumpkin for the cord. Be sure to use only light strings made for outdoor use if your totem pole is to be placed outside.

Indian Doll
By Mildred K. Zibulka

Cut an Indian costume from brown cloth. Fringe the ends. Drape it over a medium-sized plastic detergent bottle. Cut plastic arms and hands from another bottle, and attach to the sides of the doll with safety pins. Use glue to fasten together the sleeves and sides of the costume and to add colored bands of tape or tiny rickrack.

Dried cantaloupe seeds, strung together with needle and thread, make a necklace; or small glass beads can be used.

The head is a 2-inch styrofoam ball. Use sequins or circles of colored paper for the mouth. Glue the head to the top of the bottle. Make black yarn braids and tie the ends with yarn bows. Attach the braids to the head with a cloth band. Stick a paper feather into the band at the back of the head.

Witchkins and Catkins
By Beatrice Bachrach

Witchkins are witches with pumpkin heads; catkins are Halloween cats with pumpkin heads. You will have fun making them. Cut out pumpkin shapes from orange construction paper. Use black construction paper to make bodies, hats, brooms, stringy hair, and whatever other features you wish to add.

Big Eyes for Halloween
By Lee Lindeman

Glue two small paper plates together, side by side. Draw and paint a large eye on each plate.

Hold the eyes up to your face and use a crayon to mark a place to cut two small holes or slits to look through. Cut the holes out carefully.

Glue an old pair of sunglasses or frames to the back of your big eyes so they will be easy to wear.

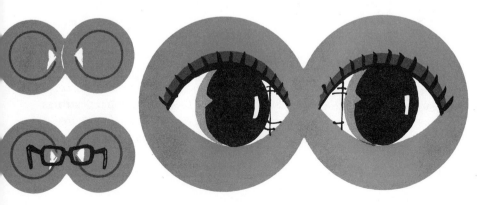

Paper Bag Costumes
By Lynn Wasnak

To make the lion suit, get a large grocery bag that will go over your head and reach down to your waist. If the bag is not long enough, you can cut the bottom out of another one the same size and glue the cut bag onto the whole one.

Put the bag over your head. Feel through the bag and mark a crayon circle on the front where your face is. Don't poke too hard. Take the bag off and cut out the circle. Make two smaller holes in front, lower down, to stick your hands through. With red and yellow crayons, make a furry mane around the face hole. On the back, fasten a tail made of rag or yarn.

For the body of the robot costume, draw a circle on the bottom of a grocery bag. Cut it out and try it on. Your head should stick out through the hole. Make armholes in the sides. Use a smaller paper bag for the head. Cut off the open end so that the bag sets well on your head. Mark with crayon where your eyes and mouth are. Cut out circle eyes and a square mouth. Decorate the head and body with crayons.

Halloween Centerpiece and Favors

By Ella L. Langenberg

Use a pumpkin as a centerpiece. Cut the face, or paste on features cut from black and white paper.

Have a face on two sides so there is no "back" for anyone at the table.

Make a scarecrow favor for each person. Cut white paper faces. Paste on black features, or crayon them. From black paper, cut hats and suits with gay dancing legs and arms. Make them look funny. Cut and paste on white buttons, and slashed yellow paper to represent straw. Fasten these scarecrow parts to pipe cleaners with transparent gummed tape.

Tape these favors all around the pumpkin centerpiece. Give each person a small safety pin to fasten the favor to coat or dress.

A Box Costume

By Lee Lindeman

A monster costume, an Indian costume, a robot costume, or a creature from outer space—all can be created from cardboard boxes. One box should be large enough to fit over your body, the other over your head.

Cut holes for your head and arms in the big box, and eyeholes in the small box. Paint with poster paint to cover any advertising.

Feathers, pie plates, paper cups, curled paper, cloth, and yarn can be glued to the boxes for costume details. Buttons, belts, badges, or shoulder patches can also be used. Why not create your own costume for Halloween?

Happy Halloween Basket

By Sandra E. Csippan

This little basket, filled with candy or cookies, is nice for a party table. Cut a piece of cardboard tube about 3 inches long. Scallop the edges of a small oatmeal carton lid. Cut two tabs from lightweight cardboard, and use them to attach tube to lid as shown. Cut a long strip for the handle, and glue the ends to the inside top of the tube.

Paint the basket. After it is dry, paint facial features with black paint or a felt pen, and decorate with other designs.

3-D Spooky Creatures

By Jerome C. Brown

Cut a circle from a square of paper by rounding the corners—any size. Use any color.

Decide on the creature to be created. Paste on facial features, hair, ears, and whatever else is needed. When dry, slit the face up the center. Overlap and paste it to give it a 3-D effect.

6

Pine Cone and Plaster Picture By Helen A. Thomas

Mix plaster of paris and pour it into a shallow plastic container. Plaster will not stick to plastic so it makes a good mold. Working quickly on the surface of the plas-ter, arrange pine cones, nuts, twigs, or pods.

If color is desired, food coloring may be added when mixing the plaster.

Pipe-Cleaner and Bottle-Cap Fun By Lee Lindeman

You will need bottle caps, pipe cleaners, stiff paper, and glue to make these fun characters.

Glue half of a pipe cleaner on the cork side of the bottle cap for a leg, and the other half for the other leg. Add two short pieces as arms, and an even shorter piece as the neck. To hold them in place, glue on an-other bottle cap, taping the two caps together until they dry thoroughly.

From the stiff paper or card-board, cut a head and glue it to the pipe-cleaner neck. Cut hands and feet from the stiff paper or card-board and glue to the arms and legs.

Paint your bendable characters with poster or tempera paint.

A Collage Sunflower Picture
By Ella L. Langenberg

This picture is made on a white paper background. Tissue paper colors show up better on white. One color laid over another makes a third color. Several colors overlaid make still another color. A color is deepened by placing two layers of the same color together.

All shapes are cut freehand. They are more interesting than those drawn and then cut.

Many triangles or petal shapes are cut from yellow paper and pasted from a center area. A brown circle, crushed to make it bumpy, is pasted at the center. Small squares or seed shapes—tan, blue, yellow, and green—are pasted hit-or-miss at one side of the circle to add in-terest.

Leaves are made from green with lighter green or yellow pasted over only a part of the leaf. Veins are cut from a darker color. Add stem and leaves to the flower.

The fence is made from strips of crushed brown.

Strips of blue show a sky color.

If houses, cars, animals, birds, or landscapes are more interesting to you, cut those paper shapes and paste them. Your own picture is sure to be attractive.

Bat Spectacles By June Rose Mobly

Draw wing shapes on opposite sides of a paper cup, and cut them out from the top rim to the round cup bottom only. Bend them out. Do the same for the head and feet. Poster-paint in black with white features and lines. Insert pipe-cleaner earpieces at the end of each wing, bending the earpieces to fit your ears.

Paper Bag Masks By Lee Lindeman

These masks are easy and fun, too. Use a big paper bag that will fit over your head. Mark with crayon or chalk where your eyes, nose, and mouth should be. Cut these out carefully. Your mask will need hair, ears, and anything that you can think of which will make it either funny or scary.

Cut some strips of paper and curl them on a pencil or with scissors. Use this curly paper for hair, whiskers, or a beard. What about a fancy hat or some paper eyelashes? Large or small ears can be cut from construction paper and glued to the bag mask. Use your imagination to create a mask which is better than any you could buy.

Paper Mache Masks

This kind of a mask is long-lasting and can be used and painted over and over again.

Crumple up some large sheets of newspaper so that they form a wad the size of your face. Tie the wad with string to preserve the shape. Tear some newspaper into strips. Dip one strip at a time into water and place each strip over the crumpled wad of paper. It looks as if you are bandaging the face. Be sure that you cover it thoroughly.

Make some creamy paste from flour and water. Dip some strips into the paste and start bandaging the face again. Put on about three or four layers of paste strips over the whole face. Do not put strips on the back of the mask.

To mold a nose, crumple up a piece of newspaper into the size nose you want. Tape the nose on with pasty newspaper strips. When the nose is secure, rub a thin layer of flour-and-water paste all over the mask. Let the mask dry for about two days or until hard.

Remove the large paper wad from behind the hardened mask. Cut eyeholes.

Paint the whole mask one color with poster paint. When the background color is dry, paint the eyes, nose, mouth, and other details. Make some ears from cardboard and glue or tape to the head.

Shellac, varnish, or plastic spray will preserve your mask and give it a shiny surface.

Glue on yarn, straw, fur, or curled paper for hair. Cotton swabs and pipe cleaners make marvelous antennae.

You can wear these masks or you can hang them up for wall decorations.

Halloween Spectacles

By June Rose Mobly

Eyeglasses made from simple materials are an easy way to change your appearance for Halloween. Some can make you look funny, others a bit ghoulish. Most of these use pipe-cleaners to connect the lenses and as earpieces. You can bend the side-pieces so they fit comfortably over your ears.

Spider-web Spectacles

Use an egg-carton lid or lightweight cardboard for the lenses. Cut out two pieces about 3 by 4 inches, rounding off the corners. Cut a hole in each lens to see through. Make spiders from cardboard circles, cutting in around the edges to form their legs. Paint the cobwebs and the spiders black, adding yellow spots on the spiders.

Witch Spectacles

On lightweight cardboard draw the triangle shape with legs and feet. Cut out this shape in one piece, then cut two eye-holes in the witch's dress as shown. Paste on a strip of cardboard for the hat brim. Draw and paint face and features, hair, hands, and stockings in appropriate colors. Paint the rest of the witch black.

Jack-o'-lantern Spectacles

For the lenses use two jar-lid liners, or cut cardboard circles. Paint them orange to look like pumpkins. Cut two stems from cardboard, color them green, and glue one to each pumpkin. Draw black triangle-shaped eyes and nose, and a big smiling mouth on each pumpkin, coloring the inside of these features.

Goblin Glasses

Use a carton from a large tube of toothpaste. Cut eye-holes in one side, and notches in the opposite side, the entire length of the carton, to represent teeth. The eyes are white cardboard circles on pipe cleaner, and the nose is a wedge of cardboard poked into a slit in the carton. Paint a red mouth around the teeth, and the rest of the box as you like.

9

Let's Do These

Cat Favor or Decoration
By Katherine Corliss Bartow

Cut two cups from an egg carton. Trim them to 1¼ inches high. Glue them together. Cut two ears from a curved section of the carton so they cup slightly. Glue them in place.

Paint the cat black. Glue on yellow paper eyes with black centers, a red nose and mouth, and three 1-inch broomstraw whiskers on each side

Make the tail from a strip of black crepe paper 6 by 1¼ inches. Wrap it around a pencil, and glue. When dry, push both ends of the paper toward the center of the pencil. Remove this crinkly tail from the pencil and glue to the cat.

Flashlight Foolers
By Lee Lindeman

Scare your friends on Halloween with a flashlight fooler.

Use a small plastic bottle that will fit over a large flashlight. Remove the label. On the bottom end of the bottle make the face of a tiger, ghost, or witch. Use dry markers to draw the scary face. Cut off the top of the bottle about an inch from the end. Cut slits two or three inches down the sides of the bottle so it will slip over the flashlight easily.

Witch and Her Kettle
By Dorothe A. Palms

Following the pattern shown, cut the witch's body from black construction paper, making slits as indicated. Roll into cone shape, interlock the slits, and paste. Patterns are also shown for the hat brim and cape to be cut from black paper. Cut the face from white paper, and add features and hair in black pencil. Push the brim down over the cone tip. Paste the face underneath it. Paste the cape along the top edge only, 4 inches down from the tip. Bend back the points for lapels. Trim as shown with colored crushed eggshells.

The kettle is a small aluminum pie tin with the rim cut off. Bend it into shape. The liner is a circle cut from a brown paper bag. Fringe the edge and curl it over a pencil. Attach a pipe cleaner handle.

These could be used as place settings at a Halloween party, with the kettle serving as the nut or candy cup.

Halloween Mobile
By Thelma Anderson

Draw and cut out an 8-inch paper circle for the moon. Draw a 3-inch circle in the center. Draw three lines across the moon, dividing it into six equal parts.

Draw and cut out three jolly jack-o'-lanterns and three black cats. Use either colored construction paper, or white paper and color it. Draw features on the jack-o'-lanterns.

Paste moon, cats, and jack-o'-lanterns on heavy paper. When dry, cut out. Punch a small hole in the top of each jack-o'-lantern and each black cat. Punch six holes around the edge of the moon, halfway between each line.

Cut along the lines up to the small circle and halfway along the small circle. Bend the flaps down.

Using 6-inch string for the cats and 8-inch string for the jack-o'-lanterns, hang them alternately around the moon. Tie knots at the ends of each string. Hang the mobile where heat is rising, and watch it move.

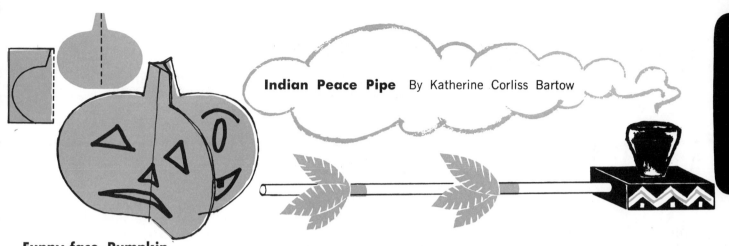

Indian Peace Pipe By Katherine Corliss Bartow

Funny-face Pumpkin
By Alice Gilbreath

Cut out three identical paper pumpkin shapes with a straight bottom as shown. Paint a different face on each. With the pumpkins folded down the center, apply glue to one half of the back of two pumpkins. Glue these together, and then glue the third pumpkin to the remaining back sections.

You can see three faces on your pumpkin by turning it around, and three more faces by holding the edges straight toward you.

Use this pumpkin as a Halloween decoration.

Hand Masks
By Lee Lindeman

Not only a mask for your face, but a mask for each hand, can make you look like a three-headed monster. You will need three paper plates.

Cut one plate in half. Place one of the halves on a full plate, face to face, and glue together at the rim. This forms a pocket for your hand. Repeat this for the second mask.

Punch holes at the top of each mask, and string on heavy yarn for hair.

Cups from an egg carton could be used for eyes. Toothpicks or pipe cleaners could be glued on for whiskers. Paint or color the masks in scary or funny colors.

The stem is a 12½-inch length of dowel. For the bowl, use a divider cup from an egg carton that has the tall, finger-shaped dividers. Cut it off at the top to 1⅝-inch height. Paint it black.

In the center of a small matchbox cover, cut a hole just large enough for the small end of the cup to fit down ¼ inch.

Glue black construction paper around the matchbox cover. Punch a small hole in the paper over the hole in the cover. Cut several slits from this hole to the edge of the hole in the cover. Push the paper inside the hole.

Cut a hole in one end of the matchbox to fit the dowel. Apply glue to the box sides and insert it in the cover. Cover the box ends with black paper. Punch a hole in the paper over the box hole, insert the dowel the full length of the box, and glue in place. Glue the pipe bowl in the hole in the cover.

Paste colored-paper Indian designs on the matchbox. Zigzag strips may be cut with pinking shears.

Glue feathers on the dowel with paper bands over the ends as shown. Feathers may be made from paper and fringed, or real chicken feathers may be used.

Owl Napkin Holder
By Sandra E. Csippan

Use cardboard tubing 4½ inches long. Draw two V-shapes, one on the front and one on the back. Repeat this on the other end of the tube. Cut out the four V's. Bend and paste on two of them for ears. Add a paper nose, and eyes with inked outlines and pupils.

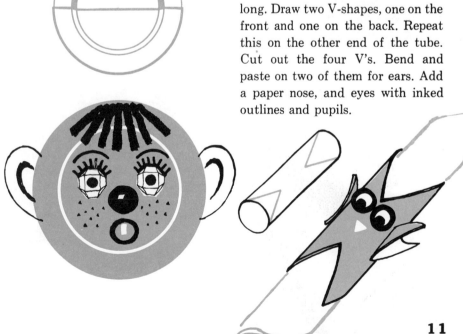

Treat and Fun Boxes
By Lee Lindeman

Cut the face of a witch, cat, moon, or pumpkin from cardboard and glue it to the cover of a small, sturdy box. Paint the face and the box with tempera.

Another kind of treat box can be made to look like a pumpkin. Paint the box and its cover, using tempera. When dry, paint or draw a different pumpkin face on each side of the box. For a stem, paint a small cork green and glue it to the cover.

Fill the boxes with treats and goodies for a party, your friends, or just yourself.

Haunted House Card   By Loretta Holz

Draw a rickety old house on black construction paper. Make it about 3½ inches high. Add windows and a front door with marker or crayon. Cut out the house.

From white paper cut out a ghost shape as shown, about 4 inches in length. Print on it PUSH UP.

Fold an 8-by-5-inch piece of colored construction paper in half. On the outside write this message: "Dear _____, on Halloween will you help me haunt a house? Look inside."

Inside put the black house with the ghost in place behind it. Put paste on the back of the house only at the sides. Be sure the ghost moves freely. Pull the ghost down so that it is invisible until your friend follows the instruction PUSH UP.

Goblin Bush
By James W. Perrin, Jr.

For each goblin, glue together two small paper cups such as those used to serve jelly or sauce in a restaurant. Cut features from construction paper and glue to goblin. Use yarn for hair. Glue a piece of yarn to each head and tie several goblins to a branch. Stick the branch in a plastic spray-can top filled with modeling clay.

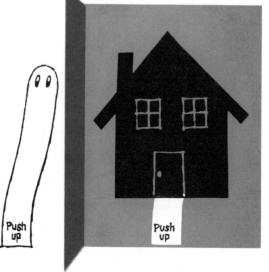

12

Scarecrow Mobile

By Loretta Holz

On a piece of scrap paper draw a scarecrow with a hat and a pumpkin face. Cut it out, separating the hat, head, shirt, and pants; and use these pieces as patterns. From double pieces of bright-colored construction paper, cut around each pattern. This will give you two identical pieces of each section. Add details with crayon or felt-tipped pen. Glue one end of the string lengthwise along the center of one pair of pants.

Add small pieces of yellow paper, cut jagged, to represent straw. Put some paste on the back of the second pair of pants and match it to the first pair. About ½ inch above the pants paste the shirts to the string in the same way, adding paper "straw" at the cuffs. Do the same with the pumpkins and the hats. Hang the completed mobile from the free end of the string.

Paper-Bag Space Mask

By Mavis Grant

Use a large, brown, heavy-duty grocery bag. Cut out an oval-shaped window big enough for you to see through comfortably. Glue a piece of cellophane paper over the opening. With crayons or felt-tip pens, draw on space designs.

The antenna is a pipe cleaner that is curled around a pencil. Push it through a tiny hole in the bottom of the bag and bend it slightly so it will not slip out. Shorten two bathroom tissue tubes and push them through holes cut in the sack where your ears would be. Slash one end of each tube to form tabs. Glue the tabs to the inside of the bag. Draw designs with felt-tip pens. Cut out a section on the sides to fit over the shoulders.

Egg-Carton Witches

By Beatrice Bachrach

From a molded-cardboard egg carton, cut a section that contains three cups arranged like two eyes and a nose. Paint white. Now paint a white face on a piece of colored construction paper. Glue egg carton section at top of face. It will blend in with rest of face. Paint remaining features and hair. Add black construction-paper hat.

Standout Halloween Paintings

By Lee Lindeman

Obtain a cardboard fruit separator from your grocer. Cut out several of the round cup-shaped discs and trim them evenly. Place them on a large sheet of paper. With a little art work, a disc can become a witch's head or a pumpkin or a cat's head or even the moon.

Glue the discs carefully to the large paper. Use tempera or poster paint to paint your picture. If the paper tends to curl up, mount the picture on cardboard.

These pictures are fun to make, and they are even fun to feel.

Elephant Mask

By James W. Perrin, Jr.

Four small, oblong, paper-mache vegetable trays are needed for this project. Cut eye-holes in one tray and cut the edges of this one with scissors in a jagged way. Trim the edges from two trays and glue at right angles to the face for ears. Cut a trunk from the center of the remaining tray. Glue in place. Paint with black or grey tempera. Add a tie made from yarn.

Jack-o'-lantern Mobile

By Nancy Alexander

Fold a 9-by-12-inch piece of paper in half and draw half of a pumpkin. Draw a smaller half inside the first. Cut out this pattern and unfold it.

Use the pattern to cut the pumpkin shape from orange posterboard. Tie a long black thread to the top of the pumpkin.

Cut a stem from green construction paper and glue it at the top, over the knot in the thread. Cut three triangles from black construction paper for the eyes and nose. Hang these in place on black threads tied through holes poked in the pumpkin. Cut a mouth from black or orange construction paper and attach it to the nose with a length of thread.

Attach a paper clip at the end of the long string, and use it to hang your mobile where it can move freely.

A Paper-plate Mask

By Lee Lindeman

On a paper plate, carefully mark and cut out the places where you want the mouth, nose, and eyes. Use cup shapes from an egg carton for the eyes, cutting a hole large enough to look through. Glue these in the eye holes.

Paint the mask with tempera. When dry, punch holes at the top. Weave thick yarn through the holes for hair.

Punch a hole on each side of the mask. Fasten a shoestring end in each hole for a tie.

Scary Halloween Cat

By Mavis Grant

Cut a large cat's head, body, and tail from black construction paper as shown. Cut three cup sections from a molded egg carton. Glue two in place for the eyes and one for the nose-mouth area. Glue on features cut from construction paper and draw on white whiskers. Push a two-prong fastener through the chin section, then through the neck. Fasten the tail to the body the same way.

You can change the cat's position anytime you like. Make him look as if he is falling, running, frightened, or just scary!

Halloween Spook Gourds
By James W. Perrin, Jr.

Paint small, dry gourds with tempera. Paint a face on the round part and use the top for the hat. Add yarn hair. Glue a band of yarn around the hair to suggest the brim of the hat. Make a small yarn pompon and glue to the tip of the hat. Glue on a yarn hanger. Cut features from paper, and glue to face.

Lion Mask
By Betty Lou Gross

The base of this mask is a 12-by-18-inch piece of orange or yellow construction paper. Hold the paper up to your face, with your nose in the center, to find out where the eyes and nose will be. (Use a piece of chalk or something else soft to mark. Never put the scissors or anything else sharp near your face.)

Cut large circles of black paper and glue down over the areas where you want your eye-holes. Cut a hole to peek through in one half of the black circle. Glue a small piece of light-colored paper to the other half of each eye. Cut a nose-hole and cover it with a flap of brown paper, glued only at the top. Make

Bouncing Black Cat
By Betty Lou Gross

Fold a large piece of black construction paper lengthwise. Make cuts ¾ inch apart from the fold to within ½ inch of the opposite edge. Unfold. Hold so that strips go up and down, overlap ends of paper, and paste. Cut ears, eyes, whiskers, tongue, feet, and tail from colored paper. Paste in place.

ears, mouth, and whiskers from black or brown paper. Glue in place. The mane is formed of rectangles of dark orange paper glued around the face.

Try your mask on again and find out where to attach the elastic. Place small squares of cardboard

Halloween Noisemakers
By James W. Perrin, Jr.

Put several metal pop-bottle caps inside a small cardboard milk carton. Cover this by pasting on a layer of paper. When dry, paint and add features. Glue on yarn hair. Force a small stick into the bottom for a handle. Put some glue around the stick to hold it in place.

at these points and staple, making the staple go through the elastic, the mask, and the cardboard square. This will make the attachment stronger.

You can use this method to make other masks, too. Try a spaceman, witch, cat, or clown.

15

For Thanksgiving

By Lee Lindeman

Soap Turkey

Use either a new or a used bar of soap. Round off the corners as shown. The bottom should be flat. This is the body of the turkey.

Cut wing and tail feathers from colored paper. Glue them to toothpicks. When the glue is dry, stick the toothpick feathers into the turkey's body for wings and a tail.

Cut two turkey head shapes from colored paper. Glue them together with a toothpick neck between. Stick the neck in the proper place on the soap body.

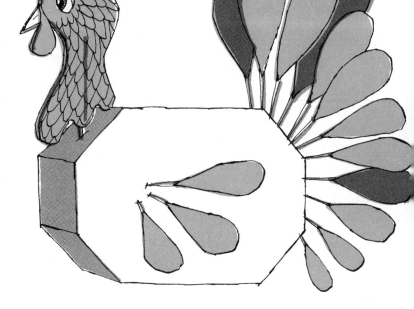

Potato Turkey

Use a fat potato for the turkey's body. Paint toothpicks for the wings and tail feathers with paint or dry markers.

For the head, use two of the cuplike shapes from a molded paper egg carton. Trim the egg cups evenly and glue them together to form a head, inserting a yellow paper bill as shown. Paint the head to match the toothpick feathers. Place a toothpick in the head for a neck and stick the other end into the body.

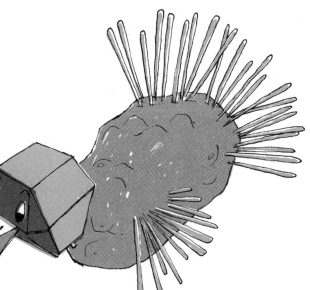

Rock Turkey

Find a rock that looks like a nice fat turkey body. Wash and dry the rock. From bright-colored stiff paper, cut turkey feathers for the tail and wings. Glue them on the rock body.

Find a smaller rock that you think looks like a turkey head. Glue it to the body with strong glue. Paint the head with poster or acrylic paint. Glue on a paper beak.

Glittering Gobbler Place Favors

By Frances M. Callahan

Help Mother with Thanksgiving preparations by making these glittering gobbler place favors. Use a styrofoam ball about 2 inches in diameter for the turkey's body. With a knife, slice off a small area so the ball will sit level. To provide a flat surface for attaching the tail, cut off a second portion of the ball's surface at right angles to the cut made for the base.

To make the tail, place one white paper baking cup inside another one and press out as flat as possible. Then fold the edge nearest you over to about a half inch from the opposite edge. With scissors, cut along the original creases in both layers of the tail to simulate feathers. Brush some white glue over the curved edges, sprinkle with silver glitter, and let dry. Attach tail to flat surface with three or four straight pins.

Bend chenille-covered pipe cleaner to resemble the shape of a turkey's head. Use either mustard seeds or tiny beads for eyes and attach one to each side of head with white glue. Attach the head to the body by pushing the end of the pipe cleaner into the styrofoam. Simulate wings by sprinkling a little silver glitter over spots of white glue brushed on each side.

Indian Tepee and Chief

By June Rose Mobly

Cut the tepee shape from the corner of a facial-tissue or cracker box. Also cut several small, thin strips of cardboard and glue them onto the tepee to represent the tent poles. Paint with tempera and, when dry, add some lively Indian decorations.

For the chief, cut off two corners the same size from the lid of a shoebox. Arrange one on top of the other, and glue together. From the flat part of the lid, cut the head and feather headdress, all in one piece. Make a slit in the center of the face and insert a cardboard nose. Glue the head section to the body. Paint with tempera.

Paper-bag Turkey   By Lee Lindeman

Stuff a small paper bag with crumpled newspaper. Tie the bag shut and fluff up the end of the bag for the tail. Cut wings from brown construction paper and glue to the body in the proper place. Cut a head from red construction paper and glue to the paper-bag turkey. Cut the tail so that it forms a feather-like fringe.

Use a cardboard tube ring for a stand. Cover the stand with a larger piece of brown paper. Cut the excess paper to form a feather-like fringe and push the feathers down and around the cardboard tube. Glue the stand to the bottom of the turkey.

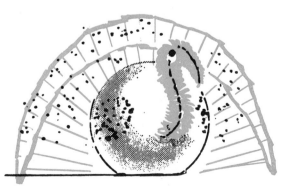

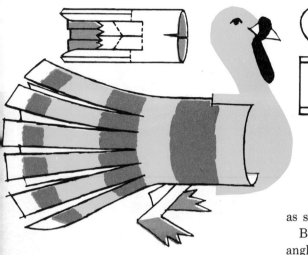

You Can Make These

A Perky Turkey

By Helen R. Sattler

Cut 2½-inch-deep slashes all around a cardboard tube at ¼-inch intervals. Leave the last two spaces slightly wider with 3-inch-deep slashes. These tabs are the legs. Cut 1 inch off each tab, then cut toe shapes on the ends. Bend these at right angles, then bend the feet as shown, 1 inch from the end.

Bend the rest of the tabs at right angles to the body to form tail feathers—except the last one on each side. Round off the ends of these and let them extend slightly behind the others to make the turkey stand.

Cut ¾-inch slashes on the front of the tube at the center top and bottom. Draw and cut out a cardboard head. Insert it into the slashes. Paint the turkey brown, leaving the tail tips white.

Turkey Nut Cup

By Mavis Grant

Cut and trim smooth one cup section from an egg carton. Paint it brown. Cut feather shapes from orange, yellow, brown, and red construction paper. Staple to one side of the cup as shown.

Cut a tiny slit in the opposite side of the cup. Cut the turkey head from red paper and push it in the slit. Fill the cup with goodies.

Make one for each member of your family to use on your Thanksgiving dinner table.

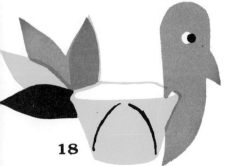

Peep Shows

By Lee Lindeman

Cut off one end of a whole cardboard egg carton, including the two eggcup-shaped parts. Glue a piece of heavy paper over the cut opening. When dry, trim off the excess paper.

Cut out the bottom of the two eggcup shapes. These holes are to look through. On the opposite side, mark a square about the size of a small postage stamp. Carefully cut out the square. This is where your picture will be viewed.

On each side of the mini-viewer cut a vertical slot as shown, about an inch long.

Cut a piece of stiff paper about 10 inches long and about 1 inch wide. On this long strip, draw and color some interesting people, designs, and scenes.

Slip the strip through the side slits and view your picture.

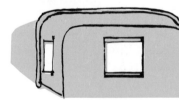

Decorated Stationery and Greeting Cards

By Ruth Foote Kingsbury

Use plain correspondence cards or notepaper, or cut 8½-by-11-inch typing paper in half and fold once.

Make your own tiny drawings; or find pictures from magazines, books, or newspapers and transfer them to the cards or notepaper. Complete them with ink, crayons, sequins, and beads.

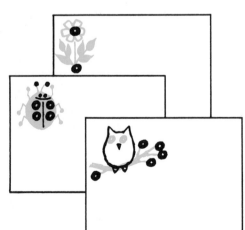

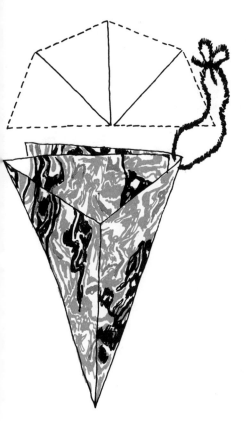

Scribble Turkey
By Mavis Grant

To make a scribble turkey you will need white paper, crayons or felt pens, one section from an egg carton, scraps of red and brown construction paper, and two beans.

On a sheet of white paper scribble circles with crayons or felt pens of different colors to make one big semicircle as shown. Leave just enough room at the bottom to draw lines for the body bottom and feet. Grass and flowers may be drawn in if desired.

Cut one of the cups from an egg carton and paste it in the center of this semicircle. Cut an oval shape from brown paper for the face and paste it over the cup. Add a construction-paper wattle and two beans for eyes.

Crayon Cornucopia
By Agnes Choate Wonson

Here is a good use for broken bits of crayon—a Thanksgiving cornucopia.

Place a wax-paper square on newspaper. Grate or shave the crayon bits all over it in a hit-or-miss pattern. Carefully lay a second sheet of wax paper over the crayon. Press very gently with a warm iron. An interesting marbled pattern is made.

Cut a triangle from construction paper. Lay it on the wax paper, creasing all around with the point of a pair of scissors. Lay the pattern on the side of the creased triangle and repeat until you have four creased triangles side by side, as shown. Cut out this shape and fold along the creases.

Lay the two outside triangles over each other and staple. Hang with a loop of gay wool yarn.

Indian Arm and Leg Decorations
By Lee Lindeman

Here is an easy and effective way to make part of an Indian costume. You will need two small paper plates, some beans or pebbles, small feathers, and a piece of yarn or heavy string about 15 inches long.

Paint and decorate the back of the paper plates. Use two or three colors for the Indian designs. When the paint is dry, glue the feathers on the rim of the plate so that the feathers extend beyond the edge of the plate.

Place a few pebbles or beans in one plate. Fasten the center of a piece of yarn or string to the center back of the other plate with a paper fastener. Glue the plates together. Be sure that the beans or pebbles do not fall out. The feathers will show around the edge of the decorated plates.

Tie to your arm or your leg for an Indian program at camp, at school, or in your club.

19

Seed Flowers
By James W. Perrin, Jr.

Collect small stems with leaves and press until dry. Glue to a piece of cardboard. Make flowers from seeds, pods, or pits. Glue in place. Add a flower stem, using a felt-tipped pen or crayon.

Thanksgiving Scenes
By James W. Perrin, Jr.

Draw a Thanksgiving scene on a piece of stiff cardboard. The important elements of your scene should be drawn on another piece of cardboard and cut out. Make your picture three-dimensional by attaching these separate pieces to the background with a piece of sponge, a paper spring, or a ring cut from a cardboard tube glued between the figure and the background.

Egg-carton Turkey Favors
By Lee Lindeman

Using the molded-type egg carton, cut and trim two cups evenly. Put glue on the rims of the cups and paste them together. This is the plump body of the turkey.

Use another carefully trimmed cup for the tail feathers, cutting a zigzag edge around the rim. Glue this to the body.

Cut the neck and head from heavy paper or cardboard and slip it into a slit in the body. Add paper wings and feet. Paint the turkey with tempera or poster paint.

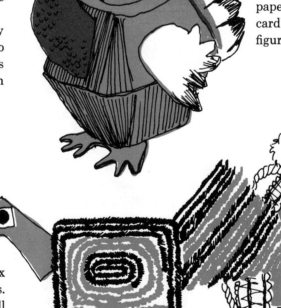

Flock of Turkeys
By James W. Perrin, Jr.

Use the contents of the scrap box to put feathers on these turkeys. The bodies are made from small boxes, Styrofoam balls, cardboard tubes, and paper cups. Use heavy cardboard for the feet and head. Paint on the features.

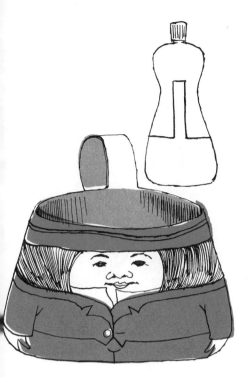

Toby Jug
By Agnes Choate Wonson

Cut the bottom 3 or 4 inches from an empty plastic bottle, leaving a strip ¾-inch wide and about 3½-inches long at the back. Curve this strip down to form a handle. Attach it to the bottle by punching two holes with a strong needle, and sewing. Or put a wire hairpin through and twist together inside. Draw the Toby figure with pen and dry marker.

This would make a good container for a small plant.

Cat Bookmark
By Katherine Corliss Bartow

Cut one cardboard cat and two black felt cats from a paper pattern. Cut off ⅛ inch all around the cardboard cat and glue it between the two felt cats.

Cut and glue in place a mouth from red paper, eyes from green foil paper, bow tie from red ribbon, and whiskers from white crochet thread.

Punch a small hole for the tail. Lay three 24-inch lengths of black embroidery thread together. Push the ends through the hole and pull them down to meet the other ends. Tie once and braid. Knot at the end. The braided tail will be almost 12 inches long.

A silver cat may be made from the metal spout of a cereal box. Lay the pattern on the flattened spout and cut out with scissors. Glue on features. Use a black tie instead of red, and make whiskers with a ball-point pen. Attach the tail.

Owl Saltbox Puppet   By Agnes Choate Wonson

Cut off a saltbox 3 inches from the top. Color it with black crayon. Cut a circle of gray felt the size of the top, cutting out the shape of the metal pouring spout. Glue felt in place. Glue a ½-inch piece of felt around the edge. Cut two triangular pieces of felt, fringe the edges, and glue in place for ears. Use white felt circles with black felt centers for eyes. Cover the pouring spout with yellow or orange felt.

By placing your hand inside the box you can make the owl's beak open and close.

Leaf Collection Characters
By Shirley Markham Jorjorian

Collecting green leaves in summer or colored leaves in autumn is an interesting pastime, especially if you can learn to identify the many different kinds you find.

To help remember each kind of leaf, make a booklet of leaf characters. Find leaves that have not been damaged by insects. Press them in a heavy book for several hours or overnight. Place a little glue on the back of the leaf and center it on a sheet of paper. Place it any way you wish to make the body of the character you have in mind. Draw face, arms, and legs. Give the character a catchy name that includes the name of the leaf. You can make clowns, animals, Martians, anything your imagination brings forth.

By using notebook paper, you can keep your leaf characters in a notebook where they will stay neat and clean.

Christmas Decorations

By Lee Lindeman

Fuzzy-Yarn Christmas Wreath

Cut out and discard the center of two paper plates. Punch many holes in one of the rings, as shown. With heavy yarn, weave in and out of the holes, leaving loops of yarn on the upper side of the ring. The loops should be about an inch high and should cover the entire area of the ring.

Glue the other ring to the back of the looped wreath. Hold the glued wreath together with clothespins, bobby pins, or clips until the glue is dry. Then cut the loops and carefully spread the end of each yarn tuft to make it fuzzy. Trim the fuzzy ends if they look uneven.

Make a bow from heavy yarn and glue it to the proper place on the wreath.

Chain Ornaments From Corrugated Cardboard

Cut 2½-inch discs from corrugated cardboard. Paint the discs and add a design on both sides with tempera or poster paint.

When dry, string them together with a long piece of yarn or colored string. The discs are easy to string if you use a longe needle with the yarn or string, pushing it through the corrugated center of each one. Use the yarn at each end to tie the chain to the Christmas tree.

A Crumpled-Newspaper Christmas Tree

From a 12-by-18-inch sheet of heavy paper, cut a very large half-circle. Form the half-circle into a cone, and staple or tape to keep the cone in shape.

Tear a sheet of newspaper into small pieces that measure about 2 inches square. Crumple up each small piece and glue to the cone with rubber cement, white glue, or a spray glue. When the cone is completely covered with small crumpled pieces of newspaper, paint with tempera paint, or spray with a spray paint. Decorate as desired.

Decorations From Slices of Tubing

By Lee Lindeman

Flatten a cardboard tube with your hand. Cut half-inch slices which, when they are opened slightly, are shaped like footballs. Arrange them in a pleasing shape such as a flower, sun spray, candlestick, or tree, and glue together. When the glue is dry, paint with tempera or poster paint. Or the slices may be painted before they are glued together.

For a pleasing, see-through effect, colored tissue paper can be glued to the back of the ornament. Put glue on the back edges of the ornament and, while the glue is still moist, press on the tissue paper. Trim off any excess tissue after the glue has dried.

For a Christmas tree, cut a long half-inch strip of thin cardboard. Bend into a triangle and glue. When thoroughly dry, glue the football-shaped slices onto the triangle.

These ornaments can be hung on a Christmas tree, in a window, or on a mobile. They can also be glued to a cardboard stand and used almost anywhere at home or school as a holiday decoration.

A variation of this idea is to use the round slices. Glue the slices together to form attractive shapes such as flowers or fruit. Paint with tempera or poster paint using bright colors. When the paint is dry, coat the ornament with two coats of lacquer or colorless nail polish for a shiny effect.

Punch two holes at the top with a paper punch. Tie a ribbon or a string at the top, and hang on the Christmas tree.

Make a Snowman By Joann M. Hart

This snowman is made entirely of heavy construction paper. For the body, cut four strips of white, 18 by 2 inches. Cross them as shown and staple at the center. Bring the eight ends up, and cross and staple them. For the head, repeat this process, using four strips of white, 12 by 1½ inches. Paste the head to the body and the body to a 5-inch-square black base, double thickness.

Cut a 4-inch circle for the black hat brim. Paste it to the head. For the crown, cut a 9-by-2¾-inch strip and a 2½-inch circle, both with tabs as shown. Roll and paste the strip. Bend in the tabs and paste them to the center of the brim. Bend and paste the small circle tabs and paste them inside the rolled strip.

Paste on black paper buttons, mouth, and eyes, and an orange nose.

Christmas Plaques
By Frances M. Callahan

Use colored paper plates, or paint them. Cut pictures from old Christmas cards. Select ones with a similar "feeling" or theme for each plate, such as the snow-and-snowman theme illustrated.

Arrange the cutouts on the plate until an interesting overall effect is obtained. Then glue in place.

Glue or tape a loop of ribbon or string to the back of each plaque for a hanger.

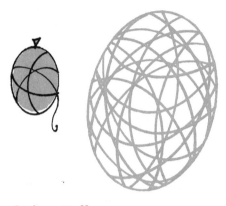

String Balls
By Lee Lindeman

Blow up a balloon and tie the end so that the air will not escape. Cut string or yarn into pieces that are as long as your arm. Soak the pieces of string in creamy white glue. Take one piece of glue-soaked string and run it between two fingers to squeeze some of the extra glue out of the string. Wrap the string around the balloon. Take another string and wrap it around the balloon. Repeat this until there is just a little of the balloon visible. Put the balloon on a piece of wax paper, or hang by a string to dry.

The next day, when the ball is dry and hard, prick the balloon. Carefully pull the balloon out of the string ball.

You can paint these string balls any color, or roll them in glue and sprinkle with glitter.

Floating Candles
By Lee Lindeman

Cut several egg cups from a molded-type egg carton. Trim each cup to make a straight, scalloped, or zigzag edge. Paint inside and outside with tempera or poster paint. When thoroughly dry, coat each cup with two or three layers of clear lacquer or colorless nail polish. Be sure to cover every surface with the waterproof polish or lacquer.

With an adult's help, melt some pieces of used candles, and carefully pour the melted wax into the small cups. While the wax is still very soft, place a small wick of heavy string down in the center. If four toothpicks are placed across the top of the cup, the wick will remain vertical while the wax is hardening.

These candles float when placed in a shallow bowl of water. A beautiful centerpiece can be created with the small floating candles.

Mantel or Table Decoration

By Margarett E. Gretchen

When using tree ornaments on evergreens, secure each ornament to a pipe cleaner. These can then be placed in any desired position or design and will remain in place.

Maccabee Dolls

By Joy F. Moss

You may want to put several dolls around the Menorah as a centerpiece for the table. Or one doll can be taped onto a place card for each guest at a Hanukkah party.

Make a loop about the size of a dime in the center of one pipe cleaner. Bend another in half and insert it through the loop of the first one. Twist these to make the head, arms, and legs. Out of cardboard, cut a tiny sword to put in one hand and a shield with the Star of David to be taped to the other hand. For the tunic, fold a 4-by-2-inch piece of cloth or tissue in half, cut a small hole at the center or the fold, and put the head through the hole. Use a piece of yarn or string for a sash. Cut a helmet and boots out of yellow paper and tape onto the doll.

Stained Glass Windows

By Marion B. Lyke

Sketch the design lightly with pencil on thin white paper. Paint the sections with watercolors. Use India ink for the outlines of the sections. When the paint is thoroughly dry, smear the entire page with salad oil.

Christmas Tree Cards From Yarn Bits

By Beatrice Bachrach

Cut and fold construction paper into a card. Draw the shape of a Christmas tree on the card front. Cut bits of green yarn about an inch long. Glue a row of the bits at the bottom of the tree. Run a strip of white glue across the tree about ¾ inch up. Place the yarn bits on the glue, allowing the ends to fall over the row beneath. Continue until the entire tree is covered. Decorate with sequins or glitter balls. Top with a large glitter ball.

Hanukkah Matchbox

By Joy F. Moss

Cover the top and bottom of a matchbox with blue felt. On one side paste a star shape which has been cut out of white felt, and on the other side paste a candle or dreidel shape. This can be used during the eight nights of Hanukkah when it's time to kindle the candles in the Menorah.

For the Holidays

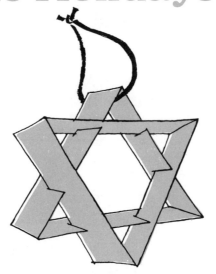

Cardboard-tube Ornaments
By Lee Lindeman

Cut a zigzag or scalloped edge on each end of a short cardboard tube. Holes can also be punched in a pattern along the edges. Paint with tempera or poster paint. The edges can be dipped into glue and then dipped into glitter. When dry, punch two holes at the top edge. Tie a string to the ornament and hang it on the Christmas tree.

3-D Star of David
By Beatrice Bachrach

Cut two equal strips of construction paper. Fold each one into fourths. Adjust the creases so that each one faces out. Next fold the two end fourths over each other to form triangles. Make two slits on each side of one triangle about a third of the way down. Insert the other triangle into these slits.

Stained-glass Windows
By Lee Lindeman

You will need black construction paper and colored tissue paper. Staple two sheets of black paper at the top. Draw an inch border around the edge of the black paper. Inside this border, outline a design or a picture with a pencil or white crayon. Instead of coloring the shapes in your picture, cut out each shape, leaving a black border around each cutout shape.

Separate the two black pieces of paper. You now have two identical cutout papers. On one of these, cover each little open space with a piece of colored tissue paper that has been cut to a slightly larger size than the cutout space. When pasting the tissue, put the paste on the black paper and then gently press the piece of tissue paper on the pasted black paper. Paste one piece of tissue paper at a time.

When you have finished covering all of the cutout shapes with tissue, replace the other sheet of black paper and staple or paste at the corners.

The stained-glass windows can be placed in a window so that the light shines through.

Trinket Tree By Shirley Markham Jorjorian

Cut three 7-inch-high tree shapes exactly alike from lightweight cardboard. Staple them together down the center. Bend each section out from the center. Paint the tree silver or green. Insert the tree trunk in a large bottle top and secure with glue or clay. Cut a ¼-inch slit on each branch to hold the ornaments.

Make small ornaments from strips of aluminum foil 1 inch wide and 3 inches long. Twist into ornament shapes around the end of a 3-inch length of thread or string. Add an ornament to the other end. Loop each pair of ornaments and put the loop into a slit. Add tiny trinkets,

wrapped candies, and gum, wrapped to resemble gift packages. Place a star or angel on the top of the tree.

A Christmas Tree From Egg Cartons

By Lee Lindeman

Cut a large half-circle from a 12-by-18-inch sheet of heavy paper. Shape a cone from the half-circle, and tape or staple to make the cone secure. Glue egg-carton cups to the cone close together so they cover the entire cone. Paint with poster paint, or spray with spray paint. Decorations of glitter, sequins, or beads can be glued to the tree. Very small ornaments may also be added.

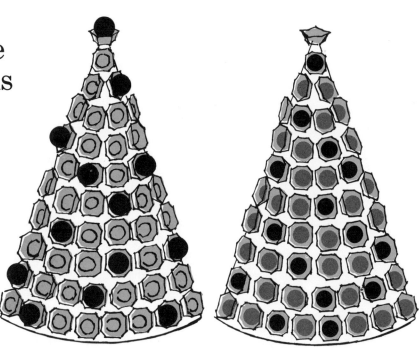

Three-piece Cardboard Christmas Tree

By Lee Lindeman

Draw and cut out a large Christmas tree from a piece of cardboard. Trace this tree on two other pieces of cardboard, and cut out.

On two of the trees cut a slit in the center, beginning at the bottom and extending halfway up the tree. The slit width should be slightly more than the thickness of the cardboard. On the third tree the slit should begin halfway up and extend to the top. The two trees having slits at the bottom must be scored from the end of the slit to the top of the tree. This is done by cutting only the very top surface of the cardboard so it will bend more easily.

Paint each tree with tempera. When dry, slip the three shapes together to form a three-dimensional tree. Decorate it with paper ornaments.

This tree can be made in any size. It also can be taken apart for easy storage.

top view

27

Gift Candle Holders
By Isabel K. Hobba

For a modern candle holder, use two empty baby-food jars. Wash the jars and soak off the labels.

Start at the top of one jar with green or brown garden-tie twine. Glue on a row at a time, round and round, until the jar is completely covered. Do not cover the opening or the bottom of the jar. Cover the other jar in the same way.

Fill one jar with sand. Use a good, strong glue on the bottom of the empty jar and around the top of the sand-filled jar. Fasten the two jars together.

You can glue three or four wrapped jars together for taller candle holders. Decorate them by gluing on paper flowers, shells, pine cones, felt, ribbon, rickrack, braid, or macaroni.

Put a fat candle in the top jar.

Easy-To-Make Creche
By Gladys O. Murry

Use a cardboard box about 6 by 8 inches. Paint the outside of the box, or cover with Christmas wrapping paper. Set it on end as shown, with the inside of the box facing you. From old Christmas cards cut figures of an angel and Joseph and Mary. Paste them to the back of the inside of the box.

On the floor of the manger scene place two small chunks of modeling clay. Press animal cookies into the clay so they will stand alone in front of the angel. Place straw on the floor in front of Joseph and Mary. Nestle a tiny plastic doll well into the bed of straw. Angels, candles or other objects can be placed at either side of the scene.

Christmas Cone Characters
By Lee Lindeman

An angel, a choir boy, Santa Claus, or even the three Wise Men can all be made from a paper cone.

Cut a piece of paper into a half-circle. Shape the half-circle into a cone and fasten together with staples or with glue. Cut off a very small amount from the tip of the cone.

Cut a head with an extra-long neck from stiff paper. Stick the neck into the narrow end of the cone and glue in place. Arms cut from paper can be glued to the sides of the figure. Shoulders or a collar may be made from a round piece of paper with a small hole cut in the center. Cut a line from the outside of the circle to the center hole. Slip the collar on your cone figure and carefully fold down on the front and the back of the cone. The collar should be glued in place.

Now you are ready to make and glue on the details. If you are making an angel you will need to make a pair of wings and a halo. A choir boy will need a music book. Santa Claus will need some cotton for his beard and for the fur on his clothes. Many of the details can be put on your cone characters with paint, crayon, or a marking pen.

These Christmas cone characters can make a wonderful table centerpiece. Small figures would make attractive place cards. Large or small, these figures make very attractive Christmas holiday decorations.

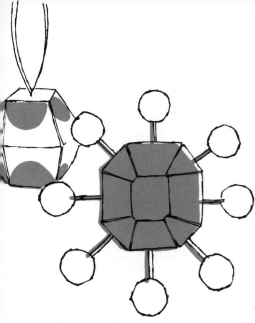

Egg Carton Ornaments
By Lee Lindeman

Cut apart the cups of a molded-type egg carton. Carefully trim each cup. Glue two cups together to create a ball form. Use a clear-drying glue, and dry thoroughly.

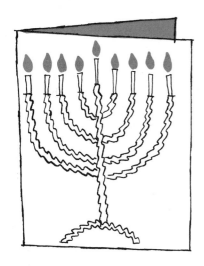

Window Picture Ornaments
By Mary L. Holmes

Use soft margarine containers and their plastic tops.

Make two small holes at the top edge of each container. Run string through the holes and tie the ends inside to form a loop hanger.

Draw and cut out from construction paper pictures appropriate

Make a pinhole at the top of each ball. Push the two ends of a 4-inch piece of string into the hole. Glue in place. Paint the ornaments with poster paint, or gold and silver paint.

Hang these tree ornaments separately, or string many of them together for a chain effect.

To make a star ornament, insert toothpicks between the glued parts. If the glue has hardened, use a pin to pierce it. Then the toothpicks should slide in easily. Beads can be glued on the ends of the toothpicks.

A glittery effect may be had by covering the surface of the ornament with a clear-drying glue, and then rolling it in glitter. Or roll the ornament in cornmeal and then paint it white for a snowy effect.

Hanukkah Greeting Card
By Beatrice Bachrach

Fold in half a sheet of colored construction paper. On the front draw a menorah with the traditional nine candleholders, starting with the center, and adding the 4 U-shapes and the base as illustrated. Glue metallic rickrack over the penciled outlines. With crayon draw the white candles and red flames. Write a message on the inside of the card.

for Hanukkah or Christmas, or cut pictures from magazines or greeting cards. Fit them inside the containers and tape in place.

Cut out the center of the plastic tops to about 1/4 inch from the edge. This makes a frame.

Place clear plastic wrap over each container, clamp the frame over it, and trim off the excess plastic wrap.

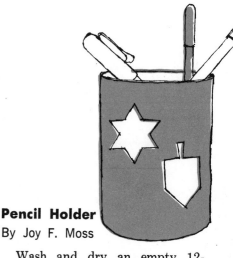

Pencil Holder
By Joy F. Moss

Wash and dry an empty 12-ounce frozen-juice can. Cut a 9-by-5-inch piece of felt or colored paper to cover the can. Carefully glue it onto the can, starting at one end and smoothing out the felt or paper until the ends meet.

Draw and cut out paper patterns of three Hanukkah or Christmas symbols. Graph paper is especially helpful when making patterns. Using these patterns as guides, make the shapes out of felt or colored paper. Glue them onto the covered can. Paper with gummed backing can also be used creatively to make this gift.

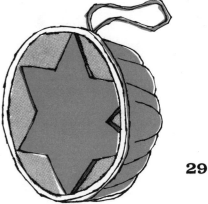

29

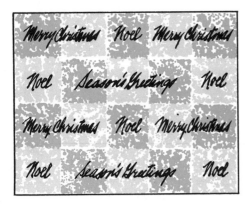

Merry Christmas Paper
By Ellen Edelman

In an old pie tin, mix green and white poster paint to a light-green shade. In another tin put plain green, not too watery. Dip a square sponge in the plain green paint, set it on a piece of white wrapping paper, and lift up the sponge. Using another sponge, make a square next to it with the light-green paint. Continue until the paper is covered with alternate green and light-green squares. When the paint is dry, use red and green crayons to write "Merry Christmas" and other messages here and there on the paper.

Dry-brush Painting
By Lee Lindeman

Use light-colored tempera paint on dark paper or dark-colored paint on light paper. Dip your paintbrush into the paint and wipe the brush on a piece of newspaper or a paper towel until most of the paint is removed. Experiment with the slightly damp brush. See the feathery brush strokes—the fluffy evergreens, clouds, and animals. Then paint your picture on the colored paper.

Make your own Christmas cards, using this dry-brush way of painting.

Snow Bottle Ornaments
By Velda Blumhagen

For each ornament you will need a clear plastic pill bottle, mothball flakes, wire or ribbon loop for the lid, and small ornaments to go inside the bottle, such as tiny colored metal balls, a small evergreen twig, a small reindeer, or a tiny creche of ceramic figurines.

Put the small ornament inside the bottle. Fill the bottle three-fourths full of water. Add mothball flakes to cover the bottom to a depth of ¼ to ½ inch. Punch a hole in the bottle lid and insert wire or ribbon loop through the hole. Make a knot underneath. Fasten the lid tightly on the bottle.

When you hang the finished ornament on the Christmas tree, a slight movement will make it "snow."

Gift Containers   By Esther C. Crosson

Cans with snap-on plastic lids make wonderful gift containers. They can be filled with candy, cookies, bath salts, hair rollers, or sewing goods.

Your mother may have such cans from coffee or nuts. Ask her to give you empty ones. They may be covered with gift-wrapping paper, wallpaper, or felt. Cut the covering you select to a size that will fit nicely around the can. Dot all-purpose glue at bottom and top edges of the can and on the part of the material that will overlap. Press material to the can.

For a handle, make holes in either side of the plastic lid with a paper punch or nail. Poke one end of a piece of yarn or leather shoelace through each hole and knot on the inside.

Candlestick Gifts
By James W. Perrin, Jr.

Glue together spray-can lids, bottle tops, and jar lids into a candlestick shape. Paint with tempera or spray paint. Decorate with strips of colored tape or strips of construction paper.

Christmas Favor
By Agnes Choate Wonson

Cut a piece of light-brown construction paper, 7 by 7½ inches. Fold it to 3½ by 7½ inches. Draw on it half a reindeer's head and the collar, as shown. Cut out along the solid lines only.

With black ink draw eyelashes and pupils, and make a dotted line up the middle of each ear. Paint the eyeballs white. Paste on two red sequins for the nose. Do the rest of the lines and shadows with dark-brown crayon. Print "Happy Noel" on the collar in black ink. Shade the letters with red crayon.

Clip or paste the collar together at A, bend the head forward at the nose, and Rudolph is ready for the Christmas party.

Cereal or Bean Christmas Wreath
By Lee Lindeman

Cut a wreath from cardboard or stiff paper. For texture, glue beans or loop-type cereal all over the cardboard wreath in an interesting design. Let it dry thoroughly. Carefully spray with paint.

Make a bow from yarn or colored paper and glue in place.

Christmas Cards
By James W. Perrin, Jr.

Cut a holly wreath, candles, and a tree from the bottom of a paper-mache vegetable or fruit tray from the grocery store. Glue to folded pieces of red construction paper. On the wreath, glue red circles, punched from construction paper with a paper punch, and glue on a ribbon bow. Add flames cut from yellow construction paper to the candles. On the tree, glue circles punched from metallic paper with a paper punch. Print greetings inside the cards.

Hanukkah Decoration
By Joy F. Moss

Make paper patterns of Hanukkah symbols such as a star, dreidel, candle, lion, or menorah. Cut these out of heavy colored paper, cardboard, or felt. Put a small hole through the top of each shape, and attach with string to a blue or white crepe-paper streamer or ribbon. You can make a 3-dimensional dreidel by cutting out two dreidel shapes the same size, slitting one half-way down from the top and the other half-way up from the bottom. Insert the bottom slit into the top slit, and make the hole at the top. The star can be made the same way.

Instead of the Hanukkah symbols, you may want to cut out the letters in "Happy Hanukkah" and attach them to a streamer.

Greeting Card Bookmark
By Agnes Choate Wonson

In the corner of a sealed envelope draw and cut out the shape shown. This opens to slip over the page for a bookmark. With a message on the back it also makes a greeting card.

Draw Santa's features on the front in black ink, completing the face and hat with colored crayon. Paste on thin layers of cotton for eyebrows and beard.

Silver Bells
By James W. Perrin, Jr.

Cut three dividers or three cups from an egg carton. Cover these with aluminum foil. String them on red or green yarn. Tie three together. These bells can be used as decorations for the Christmas tree or as a holiday pin.

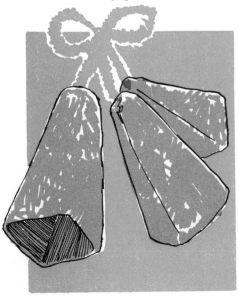

Holiday Ornaments
By Peggy Fischer

Ornaments from aluminum-foil pie pans are easily and quickly made. Draw your design on the plate and cut it out. Decorate, if desired, with glitter sprinkled on glue. Add a pipe-cleaner hook hanger as shown. The spiral is made by cutting one long continuous strip from the outside of a circle to the center.

Gold Christmas Tree Cards
By Beatrice Bachrach

Make a folder card of heavy colored construction paper. On the front paint a Christmas tree shape with gold paint. Make the ornaments by dabbing on dots of glue and adding a bit of glitter. Print a Christmas greeting inside the folder.

Paper-Towel Christmas Trees

By Lee Lindeman

From an 18-by-12-inch piece of heavy paper cut a large half-circle, and bend to form a cone. Staple or glue the cone securely.

Tear or cut a paper towel into long strips about an inch wide. Twist a strip until it resembles a piece of rope. Glue one end of the twisted paper towel to the top of the cone, wrap tightly down around the cone, and glue the other end of the towel rope to the cone. Repeat this with other twisted pieces of paper towel until the whole cone is covered.

Paint with tempera or poster paint, or with a spray paint. Small colored paper ornaments or decorations can be glued to the paper-towel Christmas tree.

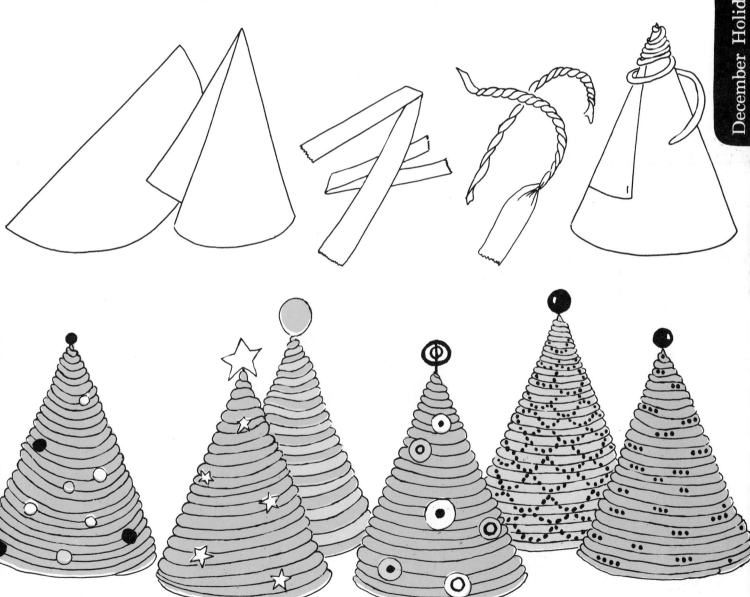

Christmas Corsages
By Blanche B. Mitchell

For the corsage, use silver ribbon with contrasting bow and wings. Cover three well-shaped peanuts with gold paint to form the heads. Glue on blue sequins for eyes, and red sequins for mouths. Arrange Christmas "angel hair" around the top and back of the heads. Shape wings of blue ribbon and glue to the backs of the heads. Point silver ribbon and catch together in the shape of a star. Add a blue bow sparkled with imitation jewels. Glue or sew the angels to the star. If preferred, six heads may be used— one for each point of the star, and one for the center.

Santa's face is one-half of a walnut shell. Paint cheeks and mouth with red poster paint. Paint a small button red for the nose. Glue it firmly to the face. Use blue sequins for the eyes. For the moustache, fringe white satin ribbon, draw it together, and glue in place just above the mouth. Make the hair and

beard from narrow lengths of white satin ribbon. Trim the red ribbon cap with a band of white velvet ribbon dotted with imitation jewels. Glue the finished head to a circle of green felt. Sew a cluster of bright ribbon at the top of the circle.

Trim gift packages with these corsages. They can be worn later. Or use them for tree decorations or party favors.

Snowflake Tree Ornament
By Dorothy L. Getchell

For each ornament paint four Popsicle sticks. When dry, glue together as shown. Weight down to dry. Cut tiny felt or bright paper rectangles and glue in place. Glue on sequins or glitter and a loop of string for hanging.

Satin Ribbon Cards
By Shirley Markham Jorjorian

These attractive greeting cards are made from half-sheets of white drawing paper folded in half and decorated with shapes cut from scraps of satin ribbon. Use white glue to attach the ribbon to the card. Extra glue can be wiped off with a damp cloth.

Plan your design first. Remember that each piece of the design must be rather narrow so it can be cut from the width of the ribbon.

Little trees may be cut from green ribbon and placed atop "hills" of white ribbon.

For a poinsettia, cut eight large leaves and eight small ones. Glue on four green leaves and a center of

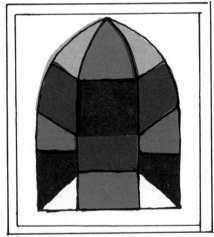

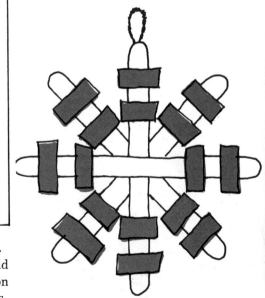

gold circles to complete the design.

The stained glass window should be penciled in first and the ribbon pieces cut from a variety of colors. When the glue is dry, outline each piece with black marker.

Santa Cookie Can
By Lola J. Janes

This cookie can is made from a 2-pound coffee can with lid, and a cardboard cover from a round oatmeal box.

Fold pink tissue paper into four thicknesses. Cut a strip long enough

to go around the coffee can, and wide enough to cover the upper two-thirds. Draw a face on the tissue with red and black crayon. Fasten the strip around the can, using gummed tape. Cover the bottom third of the can with shiny red paper.

For Santa's collar, paste a ¾-inch strip of white sparkle tissue paper around the can where the red and pink paper join. Paste on white cotton moustache, beard, hair, and eyebrows.

For the hat, cut an 8-inch circle from red paper, slit it to the center, fold it into a cone that will fit over the edge of the oatmeal box lid, and paste in place. Paste white cotton around the bottom of the hat, and a ball of cotton on the tip. Set it on top of the closed can.

Glitter Menorahs
By Beatrice Bachrach

Fold in half a 9-by-12-inch sheet of colored construction paper. Draw the brass part of the menorah with white glue, and sprinkle on glitter. Make white candles and red flames with crayon or paint.

This can be used as a stand-up decoration, or as a greeting card by writing a message inside.

December Holidays

Christmas Napkin Holder
By Beverly Blasucci

On each side of a plastic bottle draw the shape shown. The place where the shapes join must be about an inch up from the bottom of the bottle. Cut out, and discard the top part. Glue on a green felt Christmas tree shape. Decorate it with sequins, beads, tiny balls, and gold or silver rickrack. Or use your own ideas for decorating the holder. This would make a nice gift or a holiday decoration for your own table.

Plastic-bottle Angel
By Ruth Everding Libbey

Use a body-shaped plastic bottle for the angel. Cut the wings, head, and collar from a small paper plate, using the rippled edge of the plate as shown.

Draw the facial features and color the cheeks. Cut the long neck into three strips. Spread them in different directions to hold the head in place when inserted in the bottle. Paste on the neck trim.

One or more of these angels will give a Christmasy touch to your mantel.

Make a Cork Pin
By Beverly Blasucci

Cut a large cork in two. Fasten a medium-sized safety pin on the flat side with staples or nails. For the facial features use buttons, sequins, felt, or whatever seems right to you.

The Santa pin will need cotton and red felt for the hat with perhaps a little bell on the tip.

Rudolph's nose could be a tiny red Christmas ball and his ears brown felt, with a little twig or branch for each antler.

You may want to make a gift that could be used after the holiday. The funny face shown has curtain-ring earrings. The hair was made by winding yarn around the fingers, then tying it in the middle and cutting off the ends to make a shaggy hairdo.

35

Holiday Gifts To Make

Hobbyhorse
By Jane Budd

Stuff an old sock with rags or nylon stockings. Put the handle of a broom or a window-shade dowel into the sock as far as the heel. Finish stuffing around the stick and then thumbtack the top of the sock to the stick. Cover the tacks with tape.

Sew on button eyes and felt ears.

Make the mane of fringe or yarn. Heavy string makes a good halter and reins.

Wall Comb-and-Brush Holder
By Lee Lindeman

Use a small, sturdy box just large enough to hold a comb and brush. Paint the box in a favorite color.

Place the side of the box on a piece of heavy cardboard and draw a pencil line around the box. Make a design or a larger square around the pencil line. Cut out this cardboard shape and paint it with pleasing colors.

Glue the side of the box to the cardboard backing inside the pencil line with the open end of the box up. Punch a hole near the top of the cardboard so you can hang the holder on the wall.

A Houseful of Money
By James W. Perrin, Jr.

Cover a pint or half-pint milk carton with strips of newspaper which have been covered with glue. Dry. Add a tab for the chimney. Cut a slot in the roof. Paint. Add paper windows and doors.

Gift Seals
By Betty Burt

These gift seals are printed from raw potatoes and can be used to decorate packages and stationery, or to seal letters.

Cut the potato in half, crosswise. Sketch the pattern on the cut surface of the potato with indelible pencil or pen. With a knife, cut away the part that will not appear in the finished design. Do not cut deeper than 1/8 inch.

In a saucer, mix some watercolor, using a generous amount of color. The paint must be like paste rather than a liquid. With a flat brush transfer the color from the saucer to the carved design on the potato. Then print the design on gummed paper. After the designs are dry, cut out in squares, triangles, or circles, leaving a 1/8-inch margin.

String a Paperweight

By Lee Lindeman

Wash and dry a nicely shaped, smooth rock. Put a little glue on one end of the rock and wind colored string or yarn around the glue-covered end. Be sure to wind the string so that none of the rock shows between the strands.

Put more glue on the rock and continue winding until you have completely covered the rock. For a more interesting effect, use string of different colors on your paperweight.

A Handy Food Holder

By Lee Lindeman

You will need a small log or block of wood that measures about 6 inches high and about 4 inches wide.

Designs on the log or block of wood can be made with pieces of toilet tissue that you have dipped in a half-and-half mixture of glue and water. The moistened tissue is easily molded into the shape of a nose, eyes, or ears. After molding, press the shape in the appropriate place.

With a hammer and nail make about ten holes on the top of the log or block. Into these holes place toothpicks to hold pieces of hot dog, cheese, or gumdrops.

Paint the holder with tempera. Coat it with shellac after the paint is dry.

Community Bank   By Mary L. Holmes

Materials needed: 5 spice cans of different sizes if possible, enamel paints or colored construction paper, transparent tape, glue, crayons or colored pencils, one shoe-box top or long, narrow box cut down to 1 inch high for platform, 2 Popsicle sticks for tree trunks.

Make a slot in the top of each can that has none.

If using enamel paints

Roofs: Paint the top or roof of the cans black.

Sides: Paint in any building colors—gray, brown, beige, red. Then let dry.

Windows: Paint silver or white.

Doors: Paint silver or black.

Bricks: Paint two or three small ones here and there, especially around corners, in contrasting color.

Ledges: Paint a thin black line on top and bottom and across the middle.

If using construction paper

Sides: Fit the color paper you like around the cans and tape in place.

Roofs: Use black or gray paper. Fit and tape.

Windows and doors: May be drawn or colored in; or cut out small white strips of paper and glue on. Color in drapes, lamps, and bricks. Number buildings on or over doors the same as the coin to be put inside that building—1 for pennies, 5 for nickels, and so on. Tape the buildings to the platform.

Trees: Draw two tree shapes on folded green construction paper, leaving a little of the fold at top when cutting out. Open it at the bottom, paint a Popsicle stick brown and tape halfway inside each tree. Close and tape sides together. Attach the trees to the back of the platform.

37

Mini-Baskets for Candy
By Lee Lindeman

Cut the cup-shaped part from an egg carton. Cut the top edge to the shape desired. Paint the cup with tempera. When dry, glue on a handle of heavy colored paper.

Tiny designs can be drawn on the basket with crayons, pen, paint, or felt-tipped marker.

Leaf Pin
By Lee Lindeman

Find a small leaf that would be a good size for a pin. Put a thin layer of clear-drying glue on the leaf. Place a piece of paper toweling over it, and press down carefully. When the glue has dried a bit, carefully trim off the excess toweling to the shape of the leaf. While it is still bendable, shape it to look more natural. Let it dry thoroughly, then add another layer of toweling to each side of the leaf. If the natural stem has broken off, insert a piece of a toothpick with glue on the end.

Paint the leaf, using a small brush and poster paint or watercolors. When dry, add a pin back, using creamy-white clear-drying glue. Let the glue dry thoroughly, then coat with clear nail polish.

This makes an attractive dress or suit pin.

Pencil Holder
By Lee Lindeman

Use a cardboard tube about 8 inches long. Cut the tube in half the long way.

Cut a piece of stiff cardboard 9 by 4 inches. This is the base of the holder. Glue the two halves of the tube to the base, side by side, concave side up.

To make the pencil holder more useful and attractive, you can put a handle on it. Cut a 3-inch-square piece of stiff cardboard, then cut it in the shape of a circle, flower, or other design. Glue it between the tube halves.

Paint and decorate the holder with tempera or poster paint.

Decorative Spoon Rack
By Lee Lindeman

From corrugated cardboard cut an interesting shape such as a heart, circle, or square. From a molded-type egg carton, cut a section made up of four cups. In the bottom of each cup, cut a slit large enough for a spoon handle to slip through. Glue the four-cup section to the cardboard shape.

When the glue is dry, paint the decorative spoon holder with poster or tempera paint. Designs can also be added with colored paper.

Punch a hole at the top and attach a ribbon for hanging.

New Jars From Old
By Lee Lindeman

Ask Mother for a large cold-cream jar with a wide mouth and a large, flat lid. Wash the jar and cover. Collect small ceramic tiles that are left over from bathroom remodeling, or you might get some from a hardware store or a tile company.

Glue a border of small tiles on the lid as shown. Use creamy white clear-drying glue. Let it dry thoroughly. Make a design in the center of the lid with very small tiles. Put a thin layer of glue in the empty places and fill them with colored gravel, pressing the gravel down so that all the spaces are filled. Use fish gravel, or color plain gravel with food coloring.

The jar can be reused for cream, or as a container for such things as cotton or pins.

38

Make a Picture Full of Hearts

By Lee Lindeman

You will need heart patterns of various sizes, some long and thin, some short and wide, and some medium. Make them by drawing half-hearts on a fold of paper and cutting them out.

Spread out the patterns, then choose and put together on a sheet of heavy construction or drawing paper the ones that make the picture you have in mind. Or shuffle them about until they suggest a picture. Trace around them in pencil, then pencil in the center decorations with smaller patterns. Paint them with water colors or felt-tipped markers.

Or you may prefer to cut the heart shapes and the decorations from various colors of construction paper and paste them in place.

The illustrations show you how heart shapes and variations may be used but, once started, you are sure to come up with ideas of your own.

Mouse and Parasol Valentine

By June Rose Mobly

The mouse's body is a cardboard tube from bathroom tissue. Close both ends by pasting on cardboard circles. Paint or cover with colored felt or construction paper. Paste on felt or paper feet and tail.

The head is part of a pointed-end paper drinking cup or heavy paper rolled into cone shape, with features of felt or paper.

The heart and umbrella shapes are lightweight cardboard or heavy paper. Run a piece of pipe cleaner through holes punched in the body. Punch two holes in each shape. Run the pipe-cleaner end through the holes, bending the tip on the wrong side to hold the shape in place. Cover the arms with felt or paper.

The lettering on the umbrella may be crayoned or painted, or cut from felt or paper. Write your personal greeting and name on a plain white card and paste it to the heart.

String of Hearts

By Thelma Anderson

Use either colored construction paper or white paper of the same weight which you color yourself. Make several pairs of hearts, the first pair about 7 inches across, and each succeeding pair smaller. String any number you wish.

Make each heart a different color for an interesting effect. Use your imagination to decorate them. You can use glue and glitter on one side and paste aluminum foil on the other side to make them shine.

Cut a slit halfway down from the top on one heart and halfway up from the bottom on the other heart of each pair. Slide the slots together. Reinforce the slots with cellophane tape to make the hearts stay open. Punch a hole in the top and bottom of each pair of hearts and string them together with colored yarn or string. Start with the biggest and end with the smallest.

Hang them for a decoration or or mobile, or give them to a friend.

A Heart Potholder

By Lee Lindeman

Cut out a large paper heart pattern about 8 inches wide. Trace two of these hearts on a piece of heavy material such as burlap or denim. Apply clear-drying glue around the inside edge of each heart. Let the glue dry, then carefully cut out each heart. The glue helps to keep the material from fraying.

Starting at the top, sew the two hearts together with yarn or heavy thread. Before sewing the heart completely together, stuff some cotton evenly between the two hearts. Complete the sewing and tie a bow or a loop at the top of the heart with the remaining yarn.

This is not only an attractive valentine, but is also a useful gift.

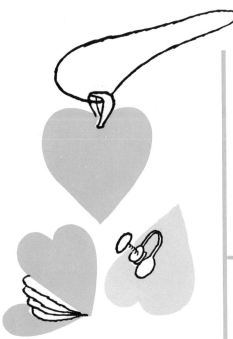

Valentine
Pendant and Earrings
By Lee Lindeman

Cut a paper heart pattern 1½ to 2 inches wide. Trace around it twice on thick material such as red burlap or denim. Go over the tracings with creamy white glue, squeezing it directly from the point of the container. When the glue is dry, carefully cut out the cloth hearts.

Put a few layers of newspaper or tissue together and cut out a slightly smaller heart. Place this padding on one cloth heart and glue the other cloth heart over it. Hold the pendant together with paper clips until the glue dries.

For a loop to put the chain through, screw in a small screw eye at the top of the pendant. Put a chain or ribbon or yarn through the loop. You could, if you prefer, sew and tie a yarn loop at the top.

For the earrings, cut two small hearts, using glue on the outline as for the pendant. Glue an earring-back to each heart.

This set makes an attractive and useful gift for Valentine Day.

Owl Valentine By Elsa Garratt

Make a heart pattern by drawing a half heart on a fold of paper. Trace and cut out four red construction paper hearts. Cut one heart in half for the wings. Paste or tape the parts together as shown. Tape the tip of the fourth heart to the back, matching it with the legs, and the owl will stand. Add two small heart-shaped eyes of contrasting color.

A Paper Valentine By Elsa Garratt

This valentine is made entirely from construction paper. Make the folder from red paper, 9 by 4½ inches. Fold it in half to 4½ inches square.

For the heart shape, fold a 3½-inch square of white paper in half. Draw the curved lines as shown in Figure 1, and cut along these lines.

Draw and cut out the arrow from a 4½ - by - ¾-inch strip of yellow paper. Cut slits along the tail to look like feathers. Insert the arrow in the heart as shown. Paste the upper rim of the heart to the folder, leaving the rest unpasted.

Write your message inside the folder.

Figure 1

Valentine Mobile By Elsa Garratt

Fold a sheet of colored construction paper in half, then in half again. Draw the design along the two folded edges (the dotted lines), as shown. Cut along these solid lines only. Unfold and pick up the outside strips at A and B, letting the rest drop down as illustrated. Insert colored string for a hanger. Push out and press down the heart-shaped cutouts.

A   B

February Make-It Fun

By Lee Lindeman

Necklace of Hearts

Use a piece of string large enough to slip over your head. From felt or stiff paper cut two hearts of the same size. Glue a heart to the string. Glue the other heart on top of the first with the string in between.

Cut out more pairs of hearts and glue them to the string in the same manner. Continue until the necklace is completely covered with hearts.

Valentines From Tissue and Glue

Cut a valentine shape from a piece of easy-to-cut white cardboard. In a cup, mix thoroughly one teaspoon of creamy white glue and one teaspoon of water. Tear or cut tissue of different colors into various shapes and sizes. Brush some of the glue mixture on the valentine. While still moist, carefully paste on a piece of tissue. Be sure all the edges are sticking. Repeat this until you have covered the whole valentine. The overlapping shapes and colors give an interesting and pleasing effect.

When the valentine is completely dry, use a black crayon or dark marker to write your message.

Yarn-Trimmed Hearts

From stiff paper or easy-to-cut cardboard cut a heart shape. With pencil, carefully draw a very simple design and border on it. Carefully put glue on these lines. While the glue is still moist, place thick or thin yarn on the glued lines, pressing it down carefully with your palm.

Easy-To-Make Ring

Save the ring from a soda can which has a self-opener. The ring should fit easily on your finger. Bend the tab so it forms a right angle with the ring itself.

Use felt, stiff paper, or a combination of the two to make a small decoration such as a circle, heart, or face. Glue the decoration onto the bent tab, and let it dry thoroughly.

Pipe-Cleaner Marionettes

Twist two pipe cleaners together to create a person or an animal. From stiff colored paper cut hearts for the hands, feet, and head. Glue them to the pipe-cleaner figure. Add details with a marker, pencil, or pen. Thread a string through the top part of the figure.

Cellophane Valentines
By Beatrice Bachrach

Fold a sheet of white construction paper in half, then in half again, giving four equal sections. Cut a fancy edge around the two open sides.

Draw a heart shape on the front and cut it out. Then trace and cut out the same shape from the section right under it. Glue a piece of red cellophane between the two sections.

Using white glue, draw scallops around the heart on the front and shake on some red glitter. Inside the folder, use red crayon to decorate around the heart shape and to write your message.

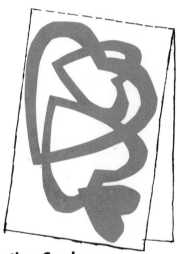

Lollipop Tree By Jacqueline Koury

Use a medium-sized juice can. With a juice can opener make V's about a half-inch apart around the top of the can near the rim. In between, make smaller V's. Holding the can opener downward from the top rim, make V's around the sides about a half-inch apart, with smaller V's in between. Spray-paint the can or cover it with white construction paper. Decorate with red sequins, ribbon, braid, wool, or rickrack.

For the tree bottom use a white plastic pint-sized container. Decorate it to match the can. Stick the bottom of the container to the bottom of the can.

Put red lollipops or peppermint sticks in the holes.

Valentine Cards
By Frances M. Callahan

The framelike hearts used for the designs are made by cutting a folded heart into strips.

Make strips by cutting off a narrow border from the curved edge of the folded heart. Repeat this cutting process until only a small solid heart remains. This will make three or more "frames." The tiny solid heart may be used in the card design if you wish.

Use a piece of construction paper folded double for the card. Arrange the heart frames in any desired design, then glue in place. Use red hearts for designs on white cards, and white hearts on red cards.

Print or write a message inside the card.

Valentines

By Ella L. Langenberg

Heart shapes may be cut freehand or as suggested in Figure 1. Figures 2 and 3 show the heart traced on a card or folder. The background is made by placing the heart in different positions and tracing around parts of it. Painting or drawing lines from the edge as in Figure 2 is one decorative idea. Another is repeating the outline with bold lines as in Figure 3. The big heart, white or red, with the message, will show up nicely against these backgrounds.

Fig. 1

Fig. 3

Fig. 2

Valentine Candy Cup
By James W. Perrin, Jr.

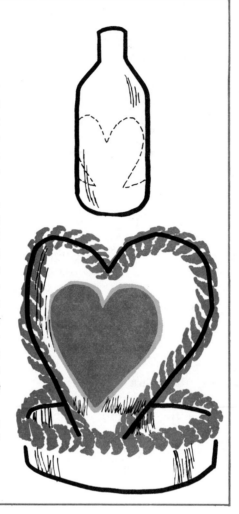

Ask mother to save an empty plastic bottle for you. Ours was clear plastic, but white or pink would be nice, too. Mark a line 1¼ inches from the bottom all around. Make a large heart pattern from paper. Snip off the bottom ¾ of an inch from the heart pattern. Place the pattern against the line at the back of the detergent bottle and draw around it. Cut around the line on the bottle and heart pattern as shown by dotted lines in the illustration. This will give you a cup with the heart shape attached, with enough thickness where they connect so the heart will stand up straight. Decorate the cup with yarn in an appropriate valentine color. Trim with paper hearts.

If you can collect enough bottles, you could make one for each place at a party or family dinner table.

Valentine Portrait
By Jacqueline Koury

Fold a strip of construction paper into three equal parts. On the middle panel paste a piece of contrasting paper slightly smaller than the panel. Next, cut out a paper heart of a third color and paste it to the middle panel. Add a nose, mouth, and eyes of scrap materials, such as sequins, pieces of yarn or braid, and pipe cleaners. Tape the ends of the paper together to make a standing frame and stand your valentine portrait on the table.

Surprise Valentine
By Loretta Holz

Cut a rectangle 1½ by 4½ inches from lightweight cardboard. Draw two lines across, one ½ inch from the bottom, the other 2 inches from the top. Fold the ½-inch section up. Cut three strips ½ inch by 1½ inches from the leftover cardboard, insert all three into the fold, and staple together near the bottom. Fold down on the other line. Now you should be able to close your valentine in the manner of a book of matches.

From another piece of cardboard, cut a narrow strip, about 4 inches long, and a small heart. Fold the long strip back and forth to make a spring. Glue one end to the center of the inside of the valentine. Color the heart red and glue to the other end of the spring.

Decorate the cover with a heart design and the words, "Just popped in to say . . ." in red crayon or marker. Write "Be Mine" in black on the heart inside. Fold the spring, close the cover, and your valentine surprise is ready to send.

Valentine Animals
By Barbara J. Smith

Draw hearts of different sizes and shapes on red construction paper. Cut out and arrange the hearts to form a variety of animals. Glue each animal to a piece of white paper. Then add details with a black crayon, pen, or marker.

Valentine Designs
By Lee Lindeman

Cut a heart from stiff paper to use as a guide. Place the heart on a piece of plain paper and draw around its edge. Now place the heart in a different position and draw around it. Repeat this until you have created a design. Try overlapping the heart shapes for an interesting effect.

Color your heart designs with paint, dry markers, crayons, or chalk.

Plastic Bottles Necklace
By Helen A. Thomas

For the pendant, cut a heart shape about 3½ inches long from a plastic bottle. Make a round hole ½ inch from the top (with a paper punch if you have one). Decorate the pendant with fingernail polish. When dry, use yarn to complete the necklace.

Pipe-cleaner Valentines
By Lee Lindeman

From heavy, colored paper cut out a valentine shape. Make a flat design from pipe cleaners. Glue it to the valentine, using clear-drying creamy white glue. Place a heavy object on top to hold the pipe cleaner design in place while it dries.

45

Four Valentine Craft Ideas

By Lee Lindeman

Valentines With Rice

Use a bright-colored paper or cardboard that will show up white rice designs. Cut out a valentine shape. Draw a very light pencil design or border on it. With a toothpick put some creamy white glue on these lines. While the glue is still moist, carefully place the grains of rice on the card to form the design. Let it dry thoroughly.

Valentine Telephone Pad

Cut about twenty white paper hearts of the same size from ruled paper, or draw your own lines. These are the inside pages for the telephone numbers.

From heavy colored paper cut a double heart joined at the top. This will fold to form the front and back covers and should be slightly larger than the pages. Staple the pages and cover together at the top.

Punch a hole near the top and string a ribbon or piece of yarn through it for a hanger.

Decorate the front cover with a telephone or valentine design cut from a contrasting color paper.

Valentine Sachets

Cut two felt hearts of the same size. Sew the two hearts together around the edge, but leave an opening large enough to insert a wad of cotton. Put three or four drops of cologne or perfume on the cotton and stuff it into the heart. Finish sewing the heart together. Cut small hearts from a contrasting color felt. Attach to the sachet with a few drops of white glue.

Weave a Valentine Design

Draw and cut out a heart on a fold of colored paper. With the heart still folded, cut out another heart from its center. Continue doing this with each smaller heart until you are down to a very tiny heart.

Paste these shapes on a piece of heavy paper, overlapping a few for an interesting effect.

In the center of each heart, punch holes about ½ inch apart with a large needle to form a design. With thin yarn, sew in and out of the punched holes.

The finished design makes an unusual greeting card.

A Heart-y Hat and Musical Valentine

By June Rose Mobly

Cut the center from a paper plate, leaving just a rim. Cut four strips of red construction paper, ½ inch wide and 12 inches long. Glue or staple to the paper rim. Also glue or staple the strips together at the point where they cross. Cut one large and several small heart shapes from red construction paper. Attach the large heart at the top of the hat. Punch holes around the rim. Use pieces of thread to hang the smaller hearts from these holes. The small hearts will jiggle when you move your head.

From a 5-by-9-inch piece of heavy cardboard, cut the shape shown, with a large heart at one end attached to a long straight strip. About 1½ inches from the end, glue on two small squares of cardboard, one on top of the other.

Paint and decorate the instrument with bright-colored paints. With felt pen or paint, add a border and the message: "Fiddle dee dee! You're the valentine for me."

Bend the valentine at the top of the heart. Cut five slits at the bottom of the straight piece and stretch a rubber band over the valentine at each slit.

Secret Message and Yarn Valentines

By James W. Perrin, Jr.

To make this secret message card, you will need two pieces of construction paper the same size, one red and one white. Fold the red paper in half the long way and cut three hearts almost all the way out, leaving about an inch at the top to hold the paper together. You can cut more heart shapes on the sides of the paper. Use white glue to attach this red paper to the white one, firmly attaching everything but the center hearts. Carefully lift each of these center hearts and write your message on the white sheet underneath.

Put the yarn on the card or the card on the yarn. Either way makes an interesting holiday greeting. The valentine-mobile is made of a length of red yarn with a bow tied at the top and five white construction-paper hearts glued on at intervals to carry your message.

Yarn designs are made by pressing lengths of colored yarn onto a line of glue squeezed out on your card in the pattern you choose. Areas may be filled in with snips of yarn pressed into white glue. These cards are made double, so you will have room to write inside.

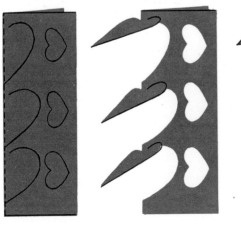

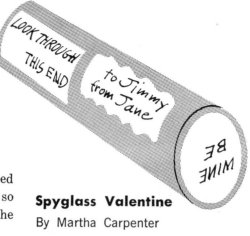

A Pin-pricked Valentine

By Agnes Choate Wonson

Cut a heart shape from a folded piece of red construction paper so that the top of the heart is on the fold.

Lay tracing paper over the folded heart and print a message to fit the card. Turn the tracing paper over so the message reads backwards.

Place the double heart and tracing paper on a piece of heavy corrugated cardboard. With a heavy darning needle or large pin, prick holes along the pencil lines through tracing paper and both hearts. This will give an interesting embossed effect on the front of the card. A paper lace edge may be added to the red heart if desired.

Spyglass Valentine

By Martha Carpenter

This valentine is made from a cardboard tube such as is found in rolls of paper towels or waxed paper. Color the tube with paint or crayon.

Make two labels, one to read "Look Through This End" and the other to read "To _____, From _____." Glue on the labels.

Place one end of the tube on a piece of tracing paper or tissue paper, and trace a circle. Inside this circle draw a heart and print "Be Mine." Cut out the circle and fasten it to one end of the tube with common pins stuck into the cardboard. The message should be placed so that it can be read by looking into the spyglass when the spyglass is being held up to the light.

Valentines With Plastic Strips

By Lee Lindeman

Cut a valentine from very stiff colored paper or thin stiff cardboard. Plan a design with a pencil, making pencil dots in the places you are going to punch holes. With a paper punch, make holes through which to weave thin plastic strips.

Thin strips can be cut from plastic bleach or liquid soap bottles. Weave strips through the holes, starting and ending at the back of the card.

String a Heart

By Lee Lindeman

Cut a heart shape from construction paper or thin colored cardboard.

Cut some heavy string into 1- or 2-foot lengths. In a cup mix one tablespoon of white creamy glue with ½ tablespoon of water. Soak the string in the glue mixture for ten minutes. Pull a piece of string through your fingers to squeeze out the excess moisture. Quickly but carefully place the gluey string in an interesting arrangement on your valentine. Carefully press the string with your fingers, and let dry. Your string design could be a border along the edge of a valentine or it could be a design in the center.

48

Five Ways To Decorate an Easter Egg

By Lee Lindeman

1. Cover the egg with vegetable coloring and let it dry. Glue clusters of tiny straw or dried flowers here and there on the egg.

2. Cut out colored-paper dots with a paper punch. Glue them to a white egg in a scattered fashion or in a design.

3. Sketch a pencil design on an egg and finish it with colored felt-tipped markers.

4. Use a blown-out egg and one or more colors of knitting yarn. Rub clear-drying glue on part of it and carefully press the yarn in position. Cover the complete egg with yarn or leave part of the egg showing through a yarn design.

5. Tear or cut colored tissue into pieces about ½-inch square. In a cup, mix one tablespoonful of water with one tablespoonful of creamy white glue. Using a small brush, cover the egg with the mixture; and press the tissue, one piece at a time, to the egg, overlapping them to cover the entire egg in a hit-or-miss design of shapes and colors. For a mosaic design, outline the pieces with a black felt-tipped marker after the glue has dried.

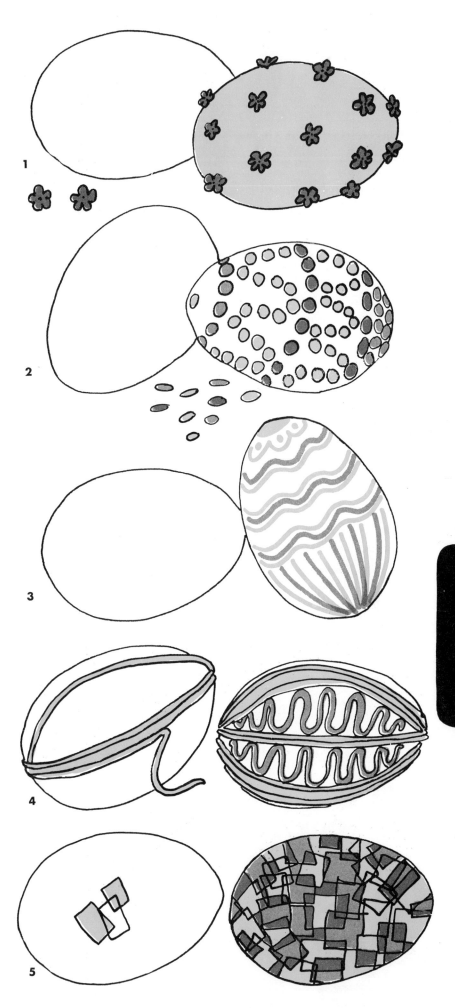

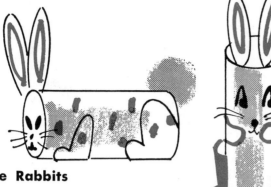

Cardboard-tube Rabbits and Chicks

By Lee Lindeman

Use bathroom tissue tubes for the body. Cut such things as legs, ears, and wings from thin cardboard or heavy stiff paper. Carefully glue them on the body. For whiskers use toothpicks, thin strips of paper, thin wire, bristles from a brush, or straws from a broom. Cotton always makes a good rabbit tail.

These chicks and rabbits can be hung in a window or used as table decorations, favors, and place cards. They can also be used in or near your Easter baskets.

Easter Hat

By Patty S. Milton

Draw and cut out a pattern of two bunny heads together. Fold a sheet of construction paper in half. Place the side of the pattern on the fold. Trace around the heads. With the paper folded, cut out the bunnies up to the fold which should be left uncut.

When you unfold the paper, you have four bunnies. This is the front of the hat. Draw faces on the bunnies. Cut a strip of the construction paper to fit around your head and paste the bunnies to it. Now you have a hat to wear on an egg hunt.

Circle Bunny and Chick

By Mavis Grant

These little creatures are made from 1½-inch-wide strips of construction paper. Each part is formed by overlapping and gluing the ends of a strip into a circle or tube shape of the desired size. The parts are then assembled and pasted together. Patterns are shown for the bunny's ears and the chick's bill and slashed tail.

How many more creatures can you make from these circles?

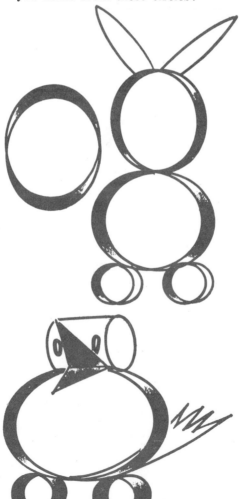

Covered Eggs

By Lee Lindeman

Carefully blow out the inside of a raw egg. This can be done by gently pricking a hole at both ends and blowing into one of the holes until all of the liquid has been removed. You can also use an egg that has been cracked in half. Fit the two halves together and tape.

In a cup make a creamy mixture of water and white glue. Tear tissue paper or paper toweling into small strips. Dip the strips into the creamy mixture and gently wrap around the egg. With a little of the creamy mixture, smooth any edges that may be standing up. Put two or three layers over the whole egg. Let the paper-covered egg dry thoroughly. If you would like some three-dimensional parts on your egg, such as eyes or flowers, dip a small piece of tissue into the creamy mixture and crush it into the shape you desire. Glue to the paper-covered egg and use small strips of gluey tissue to keep the 3-D parts securely in place.

When the whole egg is dry, paint it with tempera or watercolor paint. For a shiny and a more permanent finish, coat the dry, painted egg creation with clear, colorless nail polish.

These beautiful Easter eggs can be used for many years as decorations.

Dancing Bunnies By Joann M. Hart

Cut a piece of white paper, 6 by 12 inches. Fold in half three times to 6 by 3½ inches. Draw and cut out half a bunny shape on the fold. Don't cut the ends of the arms. This is what links the bunnies together when the paper is opened.

Cut two dresses and hair bows from contrasting color construction paper, and paste to the two girl bunnies. Cut two trouser shapes, bow ties, and pairs of suspenders, and paste to the boy bunnies. Decorate faces and clothing with crayon.

Miniature Baskets
By Lee Lindeman

Use cardboard tubes from waxed paper or paper towels. Cut the tube into small rings about 1½ inches tall. Close one end of each ring with a circle of heavy paper or thin cardboard cut to fit. Carefully trim if necessary.

Paint the baskets with poster paint and let dry. Add a handle of stiff paper or thin cardboard and small cut paper decorations. Fill with candy and nuts.

Make one for each person in your family, or enough for a school party.

Egg Carton Rooster
By Katherine Bartow

Cut two high peak dividers from an egg carton. Trim evenly and glue together for the body.

From the carton lid cut two each of feet, tail, beak, and eye. Glue these parts together in pairs, except the eyes. Paint the body and tail white. Paint feet, beak, and eyes yellow. Make a black dot on each eye. Glue tail, feet, beak, and eyes in place. Add a red felt comb and wattle. Draw on the wings with black felt pen. Trim the tail with a feather if you wish.

Topsy-turvy
By Mavis Grant

Filled with Easter grass and eggs, this makes a lovely Easter basket. After Easter, take out the grass, turn the basket over, and wear it for a hat.

Use a plain lightweight paper plate. Cut a pie-shape wedge from it. Fold the rest of the plate into a cone shape, and staple together. Decorate the cone with colored paper cups used for cup cakes. Pinch each one together at the bottom and staple or glue it to the cone, continuing until the cone is completely covered.

Using medium-weight cardboard, cut a band long enough to fit under your chin. Staple it to the sides of the cone. This band becomes the hat strap and the basket handle. If the handle has to be pieced together, cover the joining point with three paper cups to look like flowers.

Easter

51

Craft Ideas

Rabbit's Ear Ring-toss Game   By Lee Lindeman

You will need the following easy-to-get supplies: a large, round plastic bottle; a cardboard tube about 10 inches long; cardboard for the ears, paws, and legs; an 8-inch square of corrugated cardboard; and colored paper.

Glue the tube in an upright position on the corrugated cardboard base. The tube forms the body of the rabbit. Cut ears and legs from thin cardboard. Now cut two slits at the top of the tube for the ends of the ears to stick into. Cut two slits in the tube for the front paws as shown. Glue the paws into these slits. Draw and cut a face from heavy paper. Glue it near the top of the tube.

The rings can be made by gluing circular strips of heavy paper together until they are of the proper thickness. Or you can cut the rings from a round plastic bottle such as a bleach bottle.

Paint the rabbit with tempera paint. Decorate the plastic rings with permanent dry marker colors.

Make up a point system for the game. For example, a ring on an ear might be worth ten points and one on a paw, fifteen points. This game is fun to make as well as to play.

Paper Plate Hats   By Gladys Emerson

Paint or color the center back of a 6-inch paper plate yellow or orange to be the center of the flower. From colored paper cut six flower-shaped petals about 6 inches long. Paste these around the edge of the plate. Cut and paste a green leaf between two of the petals. Paste on two pieces of ribbon or tape for ties.

Eggshell Favors   By Lee Lindeman

Use an uncracked eggshell as shown. Carefully trim the ragged edge with scissors. Prick a small hole at the end of the shell.

A base can be made from heavy colored paper. With the open end down, glue the shell onto the base. Paint with tempera or watercolor.

Now put a jelly bean or gumdrop on the end of several toothpicks. Stick the toothpick ends in the hole at the end of the shell and glue in place. If you don't have candies, make some small eggs, rabbits, or chickens from paper and glue these to the toothpicks.

A Windmill   By Joann M. Hart

Cover a 9-by-12-inch sheet of white construction paper with a rainbow, using watercolors, pastels, or crayons in bright colors (no black or brown).

Make the windmill from black construction paper. Draw a line 3 inches from the bottom of the sheet, sloping the ground shape from this line. Then draw the building, and cut these out in one piece. Cut out the window in the lower part.

For the sails, cut two 1-inch strips of black paper. Fold the strips in half, lengthwise, and cut out rectangular shapes. Unfold the strips and fasten them to the tower with a two-pronged fastener, spreading the prongs on the back of the drawing so the sails will move easily.

Soap-and-Toothpick Animals By Darla Shaw

If you become discouraged carving animals out of soap, make the process easier by using toothpicks for the legs and maybe even the neck or tail. The body and head still need the use of some knife skill; but working on these two areas is not as difficult, and you'll find that the soap doesn't break and crumble as easily here.

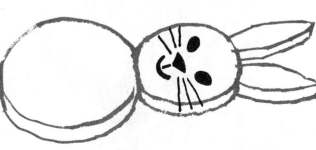

Straw Painting By Jean Tuttle Harris

You will need plastic straws, typing paper or shelf paper, and tempera or poster paint.

Dip the end of a straw into paint, stirring gently. Then hold the straw over the paper and blow. Use a different straw for each color of paint.

Continue this until a colorful design appears. This kind of painting also makes a good background design for another painting.

Be sure to cover your working space with newspaper.

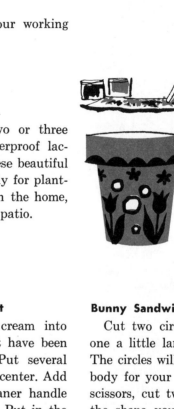

Decorated Flowerpots By Lee Lindeman

Paint a clay flowerpot a solid color, or let it remain natural. Do not paint the bottom or the inside.

Cut decorations from poster or construction paper. After gluing these decorations in a pleasing arrangement on the pot, spray or paint the pot with two or three layers of colorless waterproof lacquer or nail polish. These beautiful flowerpots are now ready for planting, and can be used in the home, on the porch, or on the patio.

Fun in the Kitchen Easter Treats By Gwen Griffen

Easter Bonnet Cookie

Put a marshmallow on top of a round cookie. Keep in place with frosting made of 3 heaping teaspoons powdered sugar, ½ teaspoon soft butter, and ½ teaspoon milk. Frost the entire hat. To decorate, cut small pieces of gumdrops with scissors. Place these around the brim of the hat in small groups to form flowers.

Ice-cream Easter Basket

Spoon softened ice cream into paper baking cups that have been set in a muffin tin. Put several small jelly beans in the center. Add to the cup a pipe cleaner handle with small ribbon bow. Put in the freezer until ready to serve.

Bunny Sandwich

Cut two circles of bread. Make one a little larger than the other. The circles will make the head and body for your Easter bunny. With scissors, cut two ears. Make them the shape you see in the picture. Spread with soft butter and soft cream cheese. With scissors, cut bits and strips of green pepper, pimento, or carrot to make the eyes, nose, mouth, and whiskers.

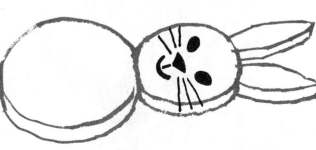

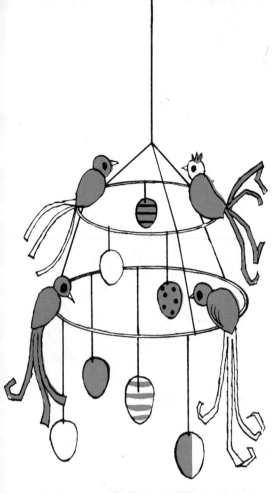

Danish Mobile
By Lee Lindeman

Use two coat hangers made from easily bendable wire. Straighten out the hangers and trim off the twisted ends with wire snippers or wire cutters. Form each hanger into a circle, one larger than the other. To keep the circle shape together, overlap the ends and fasten with thin wire or masking tape. Paint each circle. Tie one above the other, using three strings as shown. Suspend the mobile, using three strings tied to the top circle.

Cut little rabbits, birds, and eggs from cardboard or heavy paper and decorate them. Perch them on the wires, or dangle them on threads.

Chick Finger Puppet
By Mavis Grant

Use discarded cardboard tube from a roll of paper towels. Cut off a 4-inch length. Cut one end into points as shown. Paint it yellow.

Cut a diamond-shaped bill from orange construction paper and glue in place. Push a pencil through the center of the bill, turning it until the hole is large enough to fit your fingertip. Eyes may be cut from construction paper and glued on, or colored on with crayon. Real feathers may be used for wings or they may be cut from construction paper. Feet are cut from orange construction paper and glued in place.

Use your imagination to make other finger puppets.

Watercolor Pictures
By Lee Lindeman

Dip a piece of white paper into water. Let the excess moisture drip off into the sink or onto a pad of newspaper.

While the paper is still wet, brush on a few spots of color with watercolors. The color will run and mix into many unexpected forms and directions. You can imagine and see many interesting shapes and images in the running, mixing paint. Let the paint dry.

With a drawing pen or brush and India ink, draw a picture or design that encloses all of the colored splotches on the paper. Your picture could be flowers, Easter eggs, rabbits in a basket, chicks running about, or even a beautiful sky with a jet zooming into the distance.

Bunny Nut Cup
By Mavis Grant

Use the cardboard tube from a roll of toilet tissue. Cut long points halfway down the tube as shown, to form bunny ears. Glue on features cut from colored construction paper, or color features with crayons. Whiskers may be bits of string glued on. The feet are one piece of cardboard glued on the tube to form the container bottom. Add a cotton ball at the back for the tail.

54

Bunny Cards
By Beatrice Bachrach

For the bunny's ears, get tongue depressors from your doctor, school nurse, or drugstore or use Popsicle sticks. Paint them white.

On white paper draw a circle for a face. Draw eyes, nose, and mouth. Cut out. Fold a sheet of construction paper in half lengthwise. Glue the face and stick ears to the outside. Add a bow tie of cloth or crepe paper. Add bits of yarn for whiskers. Write your Easter greeting on the inside.

Cotton Bunny and Chick
By Alvera M. Lundin

Cut the body bases from heavy paper or lightweight cardboard. Cut the bunny eyes, ears, and nose from pink construction paper. Use orange for the chick's feet and bill, and black for its eyes. Crease where dotted "fold" lines are indicated.

The rest of the bodies are white cotton balls pasted to the body bases.

For the bunny, paste on four cotton feet cut like the pattern. The head, tail, and body are balls of cotton. Insert the ears between head and body, and add eyes and nose.

Finish the chick the same way.

chick base

ears

bunny base

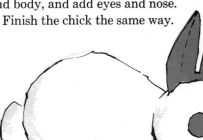

Rain-or-shine Card
By Joyce T. Buckner

The card is a piece of drawing paper folded in half, then in half again. The umbrella is made from toothpicks and tissue paper. Toothpicks can be dyed with vegetable coloring or water color paints, or colored toothpicks can be used.

The umbrella ribs are four toothpicks broken off to 1½ inches long. Glue them to the card with the broken ends together at the umbrella tip. From colored tissue paper, cut a pie-shaped wedge slightly wider at the bottom than the spread of the ribs. Trim the edge so the ribs will stick out. Put glue on the ribs. Press the cover to the two outside ribs, and then to the other ribs so the umbrella will look partly open. Put glue on another toothpick and slip it into place for the handle.

The sun is a plastic bottle cap wrapped in yellow paper. The sun rays are short ends of yellow toothpicks, glued in place.

Print "Rain or Shine" on the outside of the card. On the inside, finish the message with "I hope you feel fine."

Jelly-bean Tree
By Frances Benson

Stick some small tree branches into a flowerpot filled with earth or sand.

Push a large needle with heavy or double thread through the center of two or three jelly beans, and fasten them in a cluster. Make several clusters and tie them to the tree branches.

For the butterflies, fold colored paper, draw a wing shape with the body side on the fold, and cut out. Color them with crayons. Fasten them on the tips of the branches.

If this tree is used for a party table centerpiece, the candy may be eaten when the refreshments are finished.

Easter

55

For Mother's Day

Happy Clown
By Katherine Corliss Bartow

Cut two high peak dividers from an egg carton. Glue together as shown.

On one half glue blue paper eyes with black ink centers and eyebrows, and a red nose and mouth. Glue on raveled yarn hair. Paint the other half with tempera.

Gather a crepe paper ruff, 10 by ½ inches. Glue it around the neck. Add a front bow. Glue snips of pipe cleaner or yarn pompons down the front.

Punch holes and glue in pipe cleaner arms.

Cut a half inch from a peak divider for the hat crown. Glue it to a narrow circle brim cut from the lid. Paint the hat. Glue a feather in the crown. Glue hat onto the head.

Cut feet from the lid. Paint and glue in place.

A Living Picture
By Edna Alstrom

Use two clear plastic covers, both the same size, from food containers. Cut the outside rim from one of the covers so that it will fit inside the other one.

Pick a fresh flower with a short stem and a few leaves. Put the blossom in the center of the rimless cover, press it flat, and arrange the leaves around it.

Make the hanger from a 3-inch length of ribbon. Lay the two ends of the ribbon side by side, with the cut edges at the bottom. Crease the top fold to form a peak. Place the hanger at the center top of the rimless cover, with the cut ends extending inside about ¼ inch. Press the two covers together tightly so they will not come apart.

You can put a fresh blossom in this frame each day. When summer is over, a bright-colored autumn leaf can take the place of the flower.

Personalized Needle Case
By Katherine Corliss Bartow

This handy case is easily made from a fold of paper with an insert of felt or cloth for the needles. Old greeting cards may be used by cutting away the parts written on. Cutting with pinking shears adds a decorative touch.

Cut one or two thicknesses of felt, flannel, or linen, a half-inch smaller all around than the opened-out folder. Punch two holes at the fold, 1½ inches apart, through both paper and cloth. Run ribbon, yarn, or fancy cord through the holes and tie in a bow on the outside.

Print the name on the front of the folder. Outline the letters with white glue and sprinkle with glitter. Or add a thick layer of glue, let it dry, and paint it with thick watercolor.

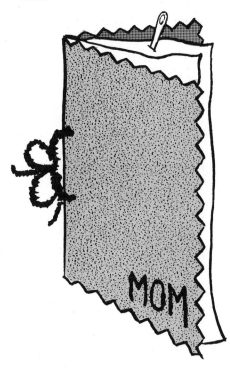

Glittery Card
By Beatrice Bachrach

With white glue, draw the petals of a flower, leaving the center area empty. Sprinkle on glitter. Fill in the center with sequins or another color of glitter. Add stem and leaves with green crayon or glitter.

Mount the picture on a fold of construction paper of contrasting color. Print a Mother's Day message inside.

Chalk Decorated Place Mat
By Christine Kandel

Using colored chalk, draw a picture on a 12-by-18-inch piece of colored construction paper. You may want to draw a landscape, a favorite animal, or a bowl of flowers. Staple clear plastic over the front and back of the picture.

A Toothpick May Basket
By Ruth Libbey

Lay toothpicks on heavy paper or cardboard in the basket shape shown. Use one toothpick for the top, one for each side, and a shorter piece for the bottom. Make the handle in the same way.

Smear some glue on paper. Lift one toothpick at a time, slide it over the glue, and carefully paste it back in place.

When the glue is dry, crisscross some toothpicks as shown to look like a woven basket. Break the ends to fit inside the basket shape. Paste in place the pieces slanting in one direction. When they are dry, paste on the pieces slanting across them.

Draw some bright flowers and leaves with crayon.

Paper Plate Wall Plaques
By Gladys Emerson

To make the fruit, mix sawdust shavings with paste—either library paste or a flour-and-water mixture with a little liquid starch added. Mix it stiff enough so that the fruit will hold its shape. Make a set of three plaques, perhaps an apple, a pear, and a bunch of grapes. Make just a half of each fruit, leaving one side flat so it will lie flat. Stick a small twig in the top for a stem. When the fruit has dried, paint it the proper color. Cut green paper leaves. Assemble together on a 6-inch paper plate. Paint a border around the edge of the plate with tempera or gold paint. Paste a piece of string on the back for a hanger.

Billy Bug
By Sandra E. Csippan

Cut five 2-inch lengths of cardboard tubing. Color four of them as desired. Use a plain color for the head piece. Paste on paper features and tongue. A coat of clear nail polish will give these pieces a lasting finish. Tie the pieces together loosely on both sides with yarn run through holes as shown. Add a fluffy yarn tail.

Creative Fun

Paper Craft Flowers By Margery Smith

Colorful paper flowers for each season can be made with colored construction paper scraps, a cork-lined bottle cap, and a little glue.

From green construction paper, cut two double-leaf shapes like Figure 1. Cross and paste them together at the center, Figure 2. Carefully remove and save the cork from the inside of a bottle cap. Glue the bottle cap upside down at center of the leaves.

Cut two double-petal shapes of a contrasting color, Figure 3. Paste together as you did the leaves. Put a little glue in the cap. Push the center of the petals into it and hold one minute. Then paste the cork into the bottle cap over the petal center, and hold firmly for another minute.

The shapes of the leaves and petals can be varied for different flowers.

Figure 1   Figure 2   Figure 3

Plastic Bottle Vase

By Alvera M. Lundin

Any plastic bottle with the same general shape as the illustration may be used. Cut the bottle evenly around as shown by the dotted lines. It will cut much easier if heated in hot water first. Cut a hole in the center of the bottom piece just large enough for the neck of the bottle to pass through. Turn the piece bottom side up and put the bottle neck through the hole. Screw on the bottle cover. Spraying or painting with gold or some bright color will add to the appearance of the vase.

Mother's Day Card

By Beatrice Bachrach

For the card, fold a sheet of colored construction paper in half. On the front, draw a snakelike line with white glue. Starting at the center, press yarn into the glue. Add stems and leaves in green yarn or crayon. Write a message on the inside.

Coasters From Yarn and Plastic

By Lee Lindeman

Cut circles larger than the bottom of a glass from the flattest and largest part of a plastic bottle. If the round piece seems to curve or bend too much, use a cool iron to press the disc between a few sheets of paper. Let the plastic disc cool under a heavy item such as a telephone book.

With a paper punch, punch holes evenly around the edge of the disc. With colorful yarn, stitch or weave around the coaster. A double row of holes could be punched around the coaster for a wider design. The yarn absorbs any moisture that may run off the glass. Why not make a matching set for a gift?

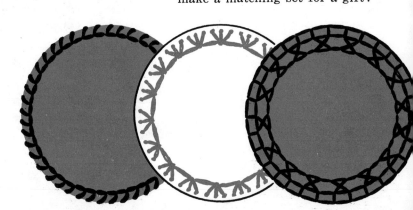

Peekaboo Cards

By Lee Lindeman

Make some Mother's Day cards with peekaboo flowers. Use stiff or heavy paper to make the card. Cut large petals from heavy colored paper. Arrange the petals into a flower on your card. Carefully glue only the tip of each petal to the card. Fold back the remaining part of each petal and write a short message to your mother under each one. Complete the rest of the card with colored pencils, crayons, or paint.

For another peekaboo card you might cut out large blossoms and glue only the bottom tip of the blossom to the card. Write a message under each blossom.

What about a tree with a message under each leaf, or a butterfly with a message under each wing? Could you make a clown with a message under each of his balloons?

Felt Pot Holder

Your felt pot holder can be any shape; round, square, flower-shaped, or fruit-shaped. The pot holder is easy to make, attractive, and useful.

Cut a pattern from heavy paper. Be sure that your holder will be large enough to protect your hand. Pin the pattern to a double thickness of felt, and carefully cut around the pattern.

Clip the two pieces of felt together. With a paper punch, punch holes that are evenly spaced around the edge of the holder. With heavy yarn, fasten the pieces together, leaving an opening so you can put in some cotton padding. Make sure the padding is evenly distributed. Then finish closing the pot holder and tie the ends of the yarn in a tight bow.

Decorate the pot holder by cutting felt shapes of a contrasting color and pasting them in place.

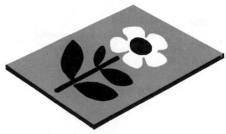

Purse Mirror

A small, inexpensive purse mirror, some small pieces of felt, glue, and scissors are the only articles you will need. Glue the mirror to a piece of felt that is slightly larger than the mirror. Carefully trim off the extra felt.

From contrasting colored felt, cut out suitable designs or decorations, and glue these in an attractive arrangement to the felt backing on the mirror.

Yarn and Plastic Jewelry

Cut one large and two small shapes from an empty plastic bottle. They may be circles, squares, or diamonds. The large shape can be used for a pendant, and the smaller shapes for earrings.

Around the edge of each piece punch holes evenly with a paper punch. Stitch yarn in contrasting colors through the holes around the edges and across the center section of the plastic shapes. Glue down the end of the yarn.

A thin metal chain can be used on the pendant, or you can make a chain by braiding three pieces of yarn together. Glue an earring back onto each small piece. The back will stick best to the yarn.

59

Pins and Pendants

By Jacqueline Koury

Aluminum lids from powdered cleanser cans may be made into attractive pins, pendants, and belts.

With a nail, hammer a hole near the edge of the lid for drawing yarn through. Then cut the lid off from the cardboard container. Remove wax or surface irregularities with steel wool, and extract any remaining cardboard before decorating.

Circles of felt, cotton cloth, or construction or fancy paper make a good background for decorations of ribbon, crossed toothpicks, pieces of felt or pie-tin aluminum, or whatever you choose.

A pin may be made by sewing a safety pin to a piece of felt and pasting the felt to the back of the lid.

A belt may be made by joining a series of lids with yarn, after making an additional and opposite hole in each lid.

Zipper Pull

By Helen R. Sattler

Mother would like to have one of these pulls to zip up the back of her dress. You will need a yard of braid or narrow ribbon, a small safety pin, and one of those little metal tab openers from a soft-drink can (or a curtain ring if you prefer).

Tie one end of the braid securely to the bottom end of the safety pin. Punch a hole in the metal tab as shown. Tie the other end of the braid through this hole.

To use, run the pin through the hole in the zipper tab of the dress, take hold of the ring on the other end, and pull.

Kitchen Creations for Mother's Day

By Beatrice Bachrach

Here's a Mother's Day card made from ingredients straight from the kitchen. Start by saving some empty jars with lids. Pour a small amount of rice into a jar. Short-grained rice takes color beautifully. Pour in a few drops of food coloring. Shake the jar and watch the rice take on color. Repeat the coloring process in a separate jar for each additional color.

Draw a vase of flowers or a bouquet. Working with one color at a time, place glue on the area to receive colored rice. Pour on the rice. Pour excess rice back into the jar. Finish with a garnish of glitter if desired.

Three-dimenisonal Cloth and Cardboard Pictures

By Lee Lindeman

From stiff corrugated cardboard cut a square or rectangular piece for a background picture base. From another piece of the cardboard cut designs or shapes and glue them in place on the base to give a three-dimensional effect.

Cut a piece of thin cloth about 2 inches larger than your picture. Put a thin layer of glue over the entire picture surface. While the glue is still moist, carefully lay the cloth over the picture. Using your fingers, rub and smooth the cloth down into the depressions and small areas as well as the large areas of your picture. The 2 inches of cloth that extend past the picture should be folded around the edge and glued to the back.

Paint the picture with tempera paint.

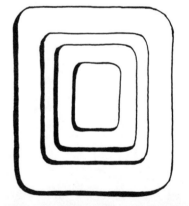

Let's Collage
By Ella L. Langenberg

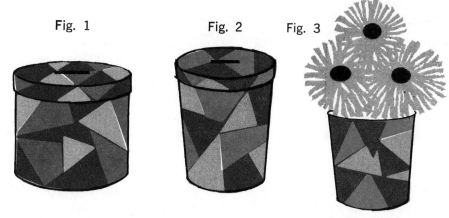

Fig. 1   Fig. 2   Fig. 3

What is collage? We have been told that it is a French word for gluing, so let us glue or paste.

Pasting paper of various kinds to make designs and pictures has been done for a long time. Real objects, such as bits of cotton, feathers, even peanuts have been glued to a background in a picture. Now many people enjoy pasting tissue paper for delicate and blended color effects, or combining strong contrasting colors for dramatic effects.

In the illustrations shown here, Figures 1 and 2 are banks for coins which are dropped through a slit in the top. Figure 1 is a cut-down oatmeal box. Figure 2 is a yogurt container. Figure 3 is a round ice-cream carton made into a flowerpot for real or artificial flowers.

All paper covering is removed and waxy surfaces are scraped and washed with scouring powder. The decoration is made from tissue paper—red, yellow, blue, green, and any other colors you wish. Strips of folded paper will cut into many pieces at one time. Triangles were used in the illustrations shown. Overlapping colors make a third color. Overlapping the same color makes it darker. Thin white paste must be used. Shellac sprayed over it will give the paper a luster.

Button Bouquets   By Gladys Emerson

Ask Mother if you may have some buttons from her button box. Choose gay colors in various sizes. Sew or glue them in place on a sheet of construction paper to make a pleasing bouquet.

Draw green crayon stems. Cut leaves from green construction paper and fold them in half. Paste one half to the sheet, letting the other half stand out. Add a bowl cut from colored construction paper.

Buttons may also be used as flower centers, using colored rickrack or other bits of cloth for petals.

Treasure Box   By Margery Facklam

Decorate a large cardboard box or carton with crayons, or cover it with colored paper or paint. This will be your treasure box. In it you will put all sorts of things you may need when you have found an idea for something you would like to make. Here is a list of some things you will find useful.

Shoe boxes—these make good forts, garages, or doll beds.

Orange juice cans—for telephones or towers.

Empty spools—for building, doll furniture, or "pretend" machines.

Cupcake papers—these make nice flowers when pasted on colored paper for get-well cards.

Old greeting cards.

Scraps of colored paper and aluminum foil.

Cardboard tubes from wax paper and bathroom tissue.

Bits of ribbon, string, beads, yarn, and cotton.

The treasure box is also a good place for paste, crayons, and scissors. Ask Mother for a place to keep the box, perhaps under your bed or in your closet.

You may find a good craft idea in a book or magazine. Or, when you look over your "treasures," you may have the fun of making something really original.

Mother's Day

Gnome Napkin Holder

By Agnes Choate Wonson

Cut 3 inches off a cardboard tube. Make a ¾-inch slit and insert the nose. This may be of sponge rubber, felt, or any stiffish material. Eyes are paper reinforcement rings, with half a ring for the mouth. Crayon the eyebrows, pupils, and other face lines to give a gnomish look. Add white cotton hair and a beard if desired. Open a colored paper napkin and refold it diagonally. Roll it to cone shape and insert it in the holder. Choose colors appropriate to the occasion. Stand a gnome at each guest's plate.

Egg Carton Cat

By Frances M. Callahan

Glue two egg-carton cups together as shown. Cut two small triangles from another cup and glue on for ears. After glue is thoroughly dry, cut off section between ears as illustrated.

Paint black. When dry, glue on green sequin eyes, half of a red sequin for a mouth, and short pieces of black thread for whiskers.

Shape the tail from black pipe cleaner. Brush a little glue on the end of it, and insert it in a hole punched in the body.

Write Secret Messages

By Anthony Joseph

You can have fun writing notes and messages to friends with invisible ink.

One easy way to make secret ink is to cut an onion in half, poke a clean writing-ink pen into the cut part, and write your message on a clean sheet of paper. Be careful not to scratch the paper with the pen. You may need a bright light to help you see the letters you're forming. The words will disappear as the onion juice dries. To make the words reappear and to read the message, heat the paper over a candle or a kitchen-stove burner. The heat turns the dried onion juice into a black charcoal material. Ask your dad to help you with this.

Turtle Paperweight   By Katherine Corliss Bartow

Cut a turtle shape from the lid of an egg carton and paint it green. Trim an egg cup to 1⅛ inches high. Fill this cup with tiny rocks or pebbles. Glue the cut edges to the turtle shape.

Remove cork liners from soft-drink bottle caps and cut the cork in different sizes. Glue the cork pieces over the egg-cup shell, fitting the pieces together. Outline between pieces with black. Glue on sequin or tiny bead eyes.

Litter Bags for the Car

By Lee Lindeman

This easy-to-make litter bag would be very useful to anyone who owns a car. You will need a medium-sized brown paper bag that is smooth and new. Around the top of the bag paste a 2-inch-wide strip of colored heavy paper. This collar will make the top a little stronger. Punch two holes about 2 inches apart on the paper collar. String a shoestring through the holes and tie the ends together in a bow.

Designs can be painted on with poster paint or watercolor paint. Crayons and dry markers can also be used to make your litter bag attractive and different.

Picnic Place Mats

By Lee Lindeman

Fold a paper towel in half and moisten thoroughly with water. Squeeze out the excess moisture carefully. Unfold the towel and smooth flat. Fold in half. Fold in half again. Then fold the folded paper into a triangle as shown.

The folded point is the center of the place mat and this is where the design begins. With brush and watercolors, paint curved and zig-zag lines across the folded paper. Add dots or other lines to complete the design, including the end border. The watercolors will spread slightly and soak through most of the layers. Carefully unfold one part of the folded paper to see if the colors are soaking through. If they are not going through enough, keep this fold open and repeat the painting over the same lines. Open another fold and repeat the painting, being sure to follow the same lines that you first painted. Use one color for the design, or many colors.

When you have finished painting, open the place mat and let it dry on a flat surface. If there are too many wrinkles, it can be pressed with a cool iron.

These place mats can be used on picnics, at camp, or at home.

Sand Casting at the Beach

By Lee Lindeman

The beach is the best place for making a sand casting. You will need a sand pail and some dry plaster of paris.

Dig an impression in wet sand, such as a crab, turtle, fish, or shell. Make the impression about an inch deep and about the size of your hand or a little larger.

Fill the pail half full of water. Sprinkle plaster of paris into the water until there is a small mound on the water. Carefully stir the mixture with a stick or spoon to release any air bubbles. The mixture should be as thick as melted ice cream.

Carefully pour the plaster mixture into the impression in the sand. Do not touch this plaster cast until it feels warm and is dull in appearance. This should happen in about fifteen minutes. Do not try to remove the cast for about fifteen minutes. Then dig away some of the sand and carefully lift out the cast. Wash off most of the extra loose sand. These casts are fragile and must be handled carefully.

Year Round

Wallpaper Animal

By Gladys Emerson

From wallpaper scraps cut circles for the head and body, and strips for the legs and neck. Cut ear and tail shapes. Paste all of the pieces in place on white paper. Crayon or paint the animal's face. Why not make a whole zoo?

Paper Plate Fish

By Gladys Emerson

Cut a small V-shape from the edge of a 6-inch paper plate. Color or paint the back of the plate. Paste on a white paper circle with a black dot in the center for the eye. From colored paper cut two large fins and a large fantail. Paste them in place. Paste a piece of string on the back for a hanger.

Octopus

By Gladys Emerson

To make this octopus you will need a paper sack, an old newspaper, some scraps of construction paper, paste, and crayons or paints. The size of the sack determines the size of the octopus.

Tear the newspaper into small pieces, wad up the pieces separately and pack them into the bag until it is as large as you want the octopus to be. Fold over the top of the sack and paste neatly.

Cut eight narrow strips of construction paper, about ½ by 11 inches, for legs or tentacles. Paste the center of each, crisscross, to the folded end of the sack. Curl the ends by rolling them around a pencil several times. Make a face on the octopus with crayons or paints. Attach a string hanger to the top so he will hang.

Bird and Fish Friends

By Texie Hering

Each duck is made from three wooden ice-cream spoons, one for the body, and two for the two wings, cut to the shapes shown. Paste one wing on the front of the body, and one on the back, like the illustration.

Each fish needs one spoon. The "pond" is a Popsicle stick with one side cut jagged to represent waves. Glue the fish to the back of the pond.

The figures may be left in the natural wood or may be painted any colors you desire. They will be easier to paint if you attach them with masking tape to a Popsicle stick for a holder.

A hanger may be made from a small square of heavy paper, half of it pasted to the back, and a hole in the other half. A similar piece of heavy cardboard makes a good stand.

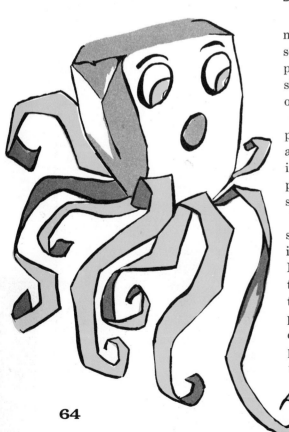

Petal Pictures By Dorothy G. Dreher

Make yourself a picture from real flower petals! Drooping flowers that Mother is about to throw out work just fine if they're not too dry.

Use flowers of different colors. Keep the leaves to use for a green color. Spread out a newspaper to work on.

Take a petal or group of petals and press against white paper to get the color. Press harder, of course, for a deeper shade. Try taking a whole flower and painting with a broad sweep to get a different effect. Brush off what is left of the petals.

You will be surprised at the shades you get from some flower petals. Experiment! You are like a painter of olden times who had to find and make his own colors from the materials in nature.

Staple your petal picture to colored construction paper a little larger than the picture to form a frame.

Sand Painting
By Lee Lindeman

You can actually draw with dry sand, and it is different and fun. You will need a clear-drying glue and some dark-colored paper.

On the paper draw very lightly a simple picture or design. Along one of the lines in the picture put a thin line of glue. Before it dries, sprinkle some sand over the glued line and let it dry for a few minutes. Carefully shake off the extra sand. Put a thin line of glue on another part of the picture and, before the glue dries, again sprinkle on sand.

Repeat this process until you have completed your picture.

Use the leftover sand to make another sand painting.

Easy Boats
By Lee Lindeman

For the main part of the boat use a small molded paper tray that your mother gets at the grocer's. Use a Popsicle stick or a long, stiff lollipop stick for the mast. Cut a slot in the center of a small square of corrugated cardboard. Glue the mast in the slot. Glue the mast and its base to the center of the boat.

Paint the boat with a latex paint. A sail can be made from stiff paper, cloth, or even oilcloth.

Another stick can be glued to the lower part of the sail at right angles to the mast, to help keep the sail in position.

Attach a string for pulling and steering the sailboat.

Crayon Creations
By Jean Tuttle Harris

With a dull knife, chip many different colors of crayons onto a piece of shelf paper, letting the chips fall over the paper. Then lay another piece of paper on the top and press with a warm iron. Remove the top paper. When the crayon is dry, draw a design over the melted colors with a black crayon or felt marker.

65

See-through Pictures

By Lee Lindeman

Beautiful pictures can be created by using the permanent color dry markers on white or light-colored tissue paper. The tissue paper can be of any size or shape you desire. Place the tissue over a pad of newspaper. This helps to absorb ink that goes through the tissue paper.

Place the picture between two cardboard frames of the same size, and glue the frames together. The finished picture can be viewed from either side.

Tape your pictures to a window for a beautiful see-through effect.

Rubber Cement Resist Party Accessories

By Lee Lindeman

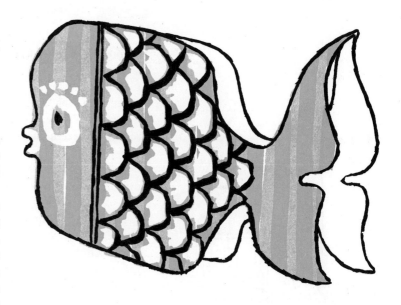

Matching party invitations, place mats, cups, name cards, coasters, and headbands can be made by using rubber cement, felt-tipped markers, and hard-finish paper such as tagboard or cardstock.

Choose a color scheme and a theme or design such as a fish, flower, bird, or abstract design. Using rubber cement and a thin paintbrush or toothpick, paint the design on the item to be decorated. When the rubber cement is dry, color the entire item with the felt-tipped markers. You may want to make stripes or zigzag lines. After the ink is dry, rub your finger carefully over the rubber cement. It will rub off easily and the design will reappear as areas of white.

Invitations

Decorate a 6-by-7-inch piece of paper with your design. Fold up 3 inches, and then fold down the remaining inch. Write your invitation inside.

Place Mats

Cut paper to place-mat size, either a rectangle, circle, or the shape of your theme. Decorate.

Cups and Coasters

Decorate the outside of paper cups. Circles of paper or your theme shape can be decorated for coasters.

Name Cards

Write the name of each guest with rubber cement on the lower half of a square of paper approximately 4 by 4 inches. Decorate. Fold in half.

A fancier card may be made by drawing the theme shape in the center of a piece of paper about 6 by 4½ inches. Decorate. Using a single-edge razor, cut out the upper half of the design so it will stand up when the card is folded in half, as shown.

Headband

Draw and cut out the theme shape in the center of a strip of paper. Decorate. Fit the headband around the head of the guest before it is cut to size and stapled.

Make a Wind Chime By Margaret Evans

A tinkling wind chime can be made from the following materials: a plastic coffee can lid, thirteen metal ends from biscuit tubes, heavy thread, and a small button.

Punch a tiny hole in the edge of each metal disc, using a small nail.

Mark and punch small holes in the plastic lid as shown.

Cut the thread into five 12-inch pieces, four 6-inch pieces, and two 15-inch pieces.

Lay aside the longest pieces. Attach one metal disc to the end of each remaining thread, and tie securely. On four of the 12-inch threads slip a disc about halfway down the thread, and tie securely (two discs on each thread).

Beginning with the center hole in the lid, slip the 12-inch thread with one disc attached through the hole. Tie a large knot. In the inner four holes do the same with each double-disc thread.

Attach the 6-inch threads to the outer holes.

Working from the top down, run one end of a 15-inch thread through the same hole with a 6-inch thread, and tie a large knot. Repeat this with the other end of the thread in the next 6-inch-thread hole. Attach the other long thread on the opposite side, in the same way.

Pinch these two loops together at the center and thread through a small button. Slide the button down and tie the two loops together above the button as shown, to form a loop for hanging. Adjust the chimes to hang straight by moving the button up or down until balanced. Hang the chimes outdoors where the breeze can blow through them, producing a musical sound.

Sponge Painting
By Jean Tuttle Harris

Draw and cut out a cardboard pattern of any object you choose. Lay it on a piece of shelf paper. Dip a sponge into tempera or poster paint, squeezing out the excess paint. Then dab at the shelf paper with one hand, holding the pattern in place with the other hand. Use a different sponge for each color. Be sure to paint around the edge of the pattern. When the paper is completely covered, remove the pattern carefully leaving an unpainted area. Decorate this area appropriately.

Mr. and Mrs. Snowman By Katherine Corliss Bartow

For each snow person, use two cups from an egg carton. Glue together. Paint white. Glue on a foam-ball head, paper eyes and mouth, red felt mittens, and a snip of yarn or pipe cleaner for the nose.

Mr. Snowman has a silver paper belt, black paper buttons, and red yarn scarf. His hat crown is the tip of one of the carton dividers. Glue it to a circle brim from the carton lid. Paint it black. Glue and tie broomstraws to a flat toothpick broom. Glue it under one of the mittens.

Mrs. Snowman's cape is 5-by-1¼-inch red felt, gathered along one edge to fit the neck. Glue red ribbon across the underside of a felt circle bonnet. Glue it on. Tie the ribbon on under the chin. Trim with a plastic or paper flower.

68

Personalized Pencil Holder By Velma Johnson

Use a round cardboard box with a removable top. Cut a circle from cloth, ½ inch larger than the bottom of the box.

Spread glue evenly over the bottom of the box, center it on the cloth, and press firmly. Slit the edge of the cloth at half-inch intervals, and glue it up onto the sides of the box.

Cut a piece of cloth wide enough to go around the box and overlap, and 1½ inches longer than the height of the box. Glue it evenly with the bottom edge of the box, leaving the extra length at the top. Smooth the cloth carefully to avoid wrinkling.

Slit the extra cloth from the edge to the box at 1-inch intervals. Glue it firmly to the inside of the box.

Cut a cloth circle 1 inch larger than the box cover. Slit at half-inch intervals. Spread glue on the outside and the inner rim of the cover. Press the cloth in place, bringing the edges over the side and onto the inner rim. Cut a circle of cloth to fit inside the cover and glue it in place.

Glue a strip of trim around the box bottom and the cover edge. Staple or sew a ribbon bow to the cover. The letters for the name may be bought at the dime store or cut from construction paper.

Snowstorm Greeting Card By Agnes Choate Wonson

For the snow, use white wool yarn, snipping it as fine and small as you can.

Make the card from light-blue construction paper about 8 by 9 inches, folded to 4 by 9—or whatever size best fits your envelope.

On the front fold draw a simple scene and complete it with colored crayon. Spread paste on areas such as the roof, and fill with the wool snow. For snowflakes, dot paste here and there on your picture and shake on the wool bits, letting them stick where they will.

The picture could have green trees with black accents, a black house with wool snow roof, yellow windows, wool snowflakes, and a dark-green border. The sloping lines and pathway in the foreground are blue, a little darker than the paper.

Fun in the Kitchen
Ice-cream Snowman
By Gwen Griffen

Put one scoop of ice cream on top of another. Use small candies or raisins for eyes, nose, mouth, and buttons. A cookie with a marshmallow on top makes a nice hat.

Puffy Pictures
By Lee Lindeman

Use a crayon to draw the shape of a large fish, flower, or face on a piece of newspaper, and cut out the shape. In the center of the shape, glue some small wads of newspaper. Around the edge put a layer of paste or glue. Turn the shape over and glue it onto a piece of cardboard. Press down the glued edge of the stuffed shape to help secure it to the cardboard. Paint your picture with tempera or poster paint.

Turnabout Puppets
By Bernice P. Smith

Make your favorite storybook characters into puppets, and make them come alive as you tell their stories. The puppets are easily made from colored paper and Popsicle sticks.

Each puppet has two faces, so cut out two of everything. Each time you glue on a part, turn the stick over and glue on a matching part.

For the head, cut out two ovals. Glue one to each side of the stick. With ink, draw a happy face on one side. The turnabout side can have a sleeping face, an angry face, or a sad face. Glue the same hair and costume to both sides of the puppet. Leave a little space at the bottom of the stick for a handle.

You might like to make some puppets for a friend who has to stay in bed. He could prop them up among the bedclothes and play "Once upon a time—"

Window Birds
By Texie Hering

Cut the head and wing shapes from a Popsicle stick, or from a double thickness of felt with heavy paper between.

The body is a pecan nut. Bore a hole in the rounded end and insert the head shape with a little glue on it. Bore a hole straight through the middle and insert a wire hairpin as shown. Use the looped top for attaching the thread hanger. Bend and spread the bottom ends for legs. Paste the wing shapes in place. Paint and decorate as desired.

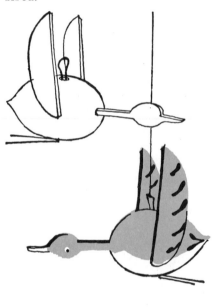

Surprise Pies
By Mildred R. Phillips

Get a paper plate like those used on picnics, and fill with gum, candy, and nuts. A small toy may also be added. Cut a piece of orange crepe paper large enough to fit over the plate. Paste in place for the top crust of the pie.

Paper-mache Danglers
By Lee Lindeman

From stiff hard paper, cut the shape of the figure or character you want on your key chain or necklace.

To make paper-mache, mix some water and creamy white glue in a cup. The mixture should be like melted ice cream. Tear a sheet of facial tissue or a couple of sheets of toilet tissue into small bits. Mix the paper and the glue mixture together.

Squeeze out the excess moisture from a portion of this paper-mache and mold it onto the stiff paper shape. Press the paper-mache carefully. Make sure it sticks to the base shape. Use very small strips of tissue to bandage the paper-mache more securely to the shape. Let the figure dry until it is very hard. Make a hole at the top of it with a needle or a pin. Do this very carefully so you don't break your creature or prick your finger.

Paint the figure with tempera paint. Use a small brush for painting the details. When the paint is dry, you might like to give your creation a shiny gloss, using clear, colorless nail polish.

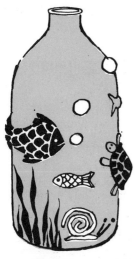

Paper-mache Over a Bottle
By Lee Lindeman

A bottle with three-dimensional decorations makes a very attractive vase for flowers. A wide-mouth bottle makes an excellent pencil holder, vase, or even a spoon holder.

Tear a sheet of newspaper into strips. Make a cupful of creamy mixture, using flour and water. The consistency of the mixture should be that of melted ice cream. Dip a strip of newspaper into the mixture, then wrap it around the bottle. Be sure it is wrapped tightly. Continue this until the whole bottle is covered, leaving the top open. Let the paper dry.

Tear toilet tissue or facial tissue into tiny pieces and add to the creamy mixture of flour and water. Let this soak for at least ten minutes. Then squeeze out the excess moisture from a portion of the soaked paper and use as molding clay. You could mold a face or a figure on the paper-covered bottle. Flowers, beetles, fish, and the like would be very interesting. Press each part of the design carefully on the bottle. If some of the larger pieces do not stick fast, bandage them to the bottle with thin strips of tissue or newspaper that have been dipped into the glue mixture. Let the bottle stand until the paper

designs are dry and hard.

Paint carefully with tempera paint. For a more permanent finish, spray or paint with clear colorless lacquer shellac.

Wallpaper Flower
By Lois Hoadley Dick

Draw and cut out a petal pattern. Tracing around it on wallpaper, cut out nine petals. Form them into a flower shape as shown, and paste together at the center. Finish with a plain color center. Paste a long green strip to the back for the stem.

Hot-dish Mat
By Lee Lindeman

You will need a piece of thin wood, heavy cardboard, or thin beaver board about 6 inches square. Glue clean bottle caps upside down in rows all over the board's top surface. Paint the board and bottle caps with waterproof paint.

From stiff colored paper cut circles that fit into the caps. A small paper design such as a flower, dot, diamond, or square may be glued onto the colored circles in the caps to make the mat more attractive. Coat the inside of the caps with colorless nail polish.

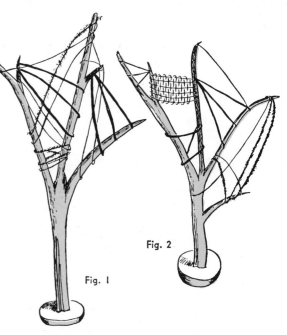

Fig. 2

Fig. 1

Spider Weaving
By Joan Walker

Pretend you are a spider making a beautiful web on a tree branch. Ask your mother if you may break a two- or three-foot branch from a tree in your yard, one with three or more little branches coming from it. Poke the branch into a wad of clay or other substance that will harden.

After this base has hardened, you are ready to have fun making a web. Weave string and yarns of varying textures, weights, and colors in and out and around and about the branches, entwining the threads as in Figure 1. Or you can do true weaving by tying many threads in one direction, and then weaving a long continuous thread in and out across those threads as in Figure 2. The finished structure will look attractive on a table or chest.

71

Soap-Powder Pictures
By Lee Lindeman

Using a pencil, draw a large simple picture on dark-colored paper. On one of the pencil lines put a thin line of glue. Before the glue dries, sprinkle on some soap powder. Carefully shake off the extra soap powder. Continue doing this until you have completed the whole picture.

Sandpaper Fun
By Marion Ullmark

Glue a sheet of coarse sandpaper to the bottom or top of a cardboard box. This will give you a raised surface to work on, and will make it easy to move your project around. Using yarn or heavy string, make an outline picture on the sandpaper. The yarn will stick to the sandpaper without paste or glue. When you wish to make another picture, just pull up the yarn and start over. Store the yarn in the box when not in use.

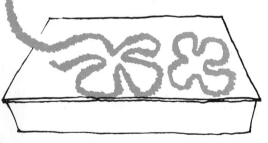

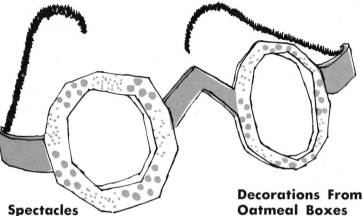

Spectacles
By James W. Perrin, Jr.

Cut the spectacle frames out of an oblong paper-mache vegetable tray from the supermarket. Paint on an interesting design or other decoration. Make lenses from clear plastic food wrap or pieces of a plastic bag and glue on. Make a small hole at each side to attach pipe-cleaner ear-pieces.

Foot Pictures
By Mavis Grant

Draw around your shoe on a sheet of white paper. Make these outlines into girls or boys or animals by adding features with crayon or felt-tipped pens. You may wish to paste old buttons or jewelry for eyes. Yarn scraps make funny hair and you may make clothes for your foot people from scraps of cloth. Arms and legs may be added if desired. Let your imagination run wild!

Decorations From Oatmeal Boxes
By Helen A. Thomas

Remove the lid from a round oatmeal box. With scissors cut the box in strips from the top down to about 3/4 inch from the bottom. Fold back the strips and shape them as you like. You can also remove some of the strips to create a different type of character.

Paint the face and strips with bright colors of tempera or other paint you have on hand. Glue it to colored construction paper that has been cut in a design to go with the face.

Fancy Frames for Pictures
By Lee Lindeman

Wash and dry a large meat tray, the kind that meat is sold in at the supermarket. Glue the tray to a piece of stiff cardboard which you have cut about 2 inches larger than the tray on all sides.

On the border around the tray, glue cups that you have carefully cut from a molded cardboard egg carton. The cups should be cut so they look like flowers. Spray or paint the whole frame with tempera or poster paint. Draw or paint a picture which will fit into your new frame.

Mr. Funnyman Noses
By Esther Norman

Cut egg cups from a paper-mache egg carton. Soak in warm water a few hours until the material is soft and pliable.

Press them around a plastic pill bottle or a piece of wood or your father's thumb, until you have something large enough to make a Mr. Funnyman nose.

Tie string loosely around them to hold the shape till they dry. Then fasten a piece of string on the sides of each nose, to tie on like a Halloween mask.

You and your friends can make enough Funnyman noses to supply a whole schoolyard of children. Think how funny you will all look, running around with noses tied on!

Envelope Puppets
By Marie Stern

Cut two half-circle holes near the middle of the bottom of an envelope. Open up the flap. Draw a person or an animal so that the head is in the flap-space and the legs stop at the knees. Now, put your index and middle fingers in the envelope and through the holes at the bottom. You can make your creature hop or dance by moving your fingers.

Colorful Hints
By Virginia Harman

When painting at an easel, try adding a little liquid starch to tempera paint. You will be pleased to find that it does not run or drip.

For an easel, art paper can be clipped with two spring-type clothespins to a large piece of cardboard. Lean the cardboard against the wall. A paperweight, flat stone, or other weighty object set at the bottom edge will hold the makeshift easel steady while painting.

For finger paint use liquid starch with tempera, making a thick paint by using very little water. And for easy clean up, try finger painting in a cookie tray. The tray can be washed easily and reused many times. If you want to save your painting, cut some finger-paint paper the right size to fit into the tray.

When painting wax cartons with watercolors, add a few drops of detergent to the paint. One teaspoonful is enough for a pint or more of paint.

For something different in a brush, and for making designs in colors, use a bit of sponge with a clamp-clothespin handle.

Save those short pieces of wax crayons and melt different colors together in a small aluminum tray such as frozen foods come in. When cooled, you will have something new and different with which to color, draw, or make pretty designs.

73

Vacation Make-It Fun

Paper-mache Cookie Keeper
By Lee Lindeman

Use an empty coffee can with a snap-on plastic lid.

Tear or cut newspaper or paper toweling into thin strips. Into a cup put one-half cup of water and one-fourth cup of flour. Mix until creamy. Dip the thin strips of paper into the mixture and wrap them around the coffee can. Be sure that all of the strips are smooth and flat against the can.

Cut details such as ears and nose from cardboard and glue them to the proper place on the can. Cover them with a layer or two of the thin paper strips.

Eyes can be made from a small wad of newspaper or toweling. Bandage them to the can with the glue-dipped strips.

Let the paper dry thoroughly. Paint with tempera paint. Finish with two coats of shellac or other clear coating.

Kat Knickknack
By Bonnie France

Make the face from a 2½ inch circle of heavy white paper. Paste on colored paper eyes and a chenille or cotton nose. Draw black crayon whiskers. Paste the face to a clamp-type clothespin as shown, with the prongs extending above the face to form ears.

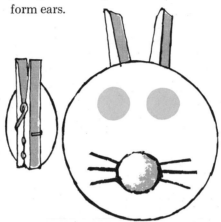

Spring Bouquet
By Judith LaDez

Cut a four-petal flower pattern, about 1½ inches across, from cardboard or heavy paper. With a pencil trace around the pattern on several thicknesses of pastel-colored tissue paper. Next make a set of larger flowers by drawing about ¼ inch larger all around the pattern. Do the same thing to make flowers ½ inch larger than the pattern. Cut all the flower shapes out of several thicknesses of paper.

To assemble the flowers, first place one of the largest petals flat on a table. On top of this, place the next size petal, turning it slightly to alternate the outer edges. Then place the smallest petal on top of these, again turning it slightly, and push a brass fastener through the center of the three layers of petal. Now attach the flower to a sheet of

Onion Sack Hat
By James W. Perrin, Jr.

The next time Mother buys a sack of onions ask her to save the bag for you. Carefully cut off the label end where it is sewed together. Beginning at this end weave yarn through the openings. Add several rows of yarn of different colors. Tie the ends of yarn together. Usually the other end of the sack is held together with a metal staple but, if it is not, tie it together with yarn.

construction paper by pushing the fastener through the paper and spreading it open in the back.

Arrange several of these flowers to form a bouquet and paste a vase cut from construction paper beneath them.

Sandcasting By Tulla Price

Fill a wooden box about half-full of sand. Smooth the sand and make a design by pushing the sand down and around. Use spoons, sticks, fingers, hands, or anything that would make an interesting pattern.

This design will be reversed in the plaster cast. The dents or low places in the sand will become raised places in the cast, and the raised places will become dents.

Fill a bowl with water and carefully add dry plaster of paris until it is as thick as melted ice cream. Quickly and carefully pour the plaster into the box, making sure not to move any of the sand. Place a loop of wire in the plaster for a hanger.

When the plaster is set, remove the cast from the box. Paint or stain the picture or design. Sandcasting is usually done in a dull finish. Dull spray may be used for a sealer if needed.

Egg Carton Octopus
By Katherine Corliss Bartow

Trim an egg-carton cup to 1 inch. Make a thread loop in the top for hanging.

From carton scraps cut a circle base to fit the cut edge. Some cartons are gray, a good octopus color. Or you can paint cup and base.

Tentacles are eight plastic- or paper-covered wire twists that secure bread wrappers. White paper ones can be painted. Glue one end of each tentacle inside the edge of the cup. Glue the cup to the base over tentacles. Dry.

Mark forehead with a ball-point pen. Eyes and mouth are paper.

Twist tentacles in lifelike positions. Hang. A mobile with each octopus painted a different color is fun.

Funny-Face Fan
By Agnes Choate Wonson

Cut a fan shape from corrugated cardboard, being sure that the grooves run vertically. From felt scraps cut out a big mouth, eyes, nose, and forehead-piece and glue them in place. In each eye, place a paper reinforcement ring. Indicate eyebrows. On each side of the temple insert about two dozen lengths of yarn. Tie a loose knot before inserting yarn in the grooves. Insert two pipe cleaners for the handle, using glue. Add a tiny cap between the hair tufts.

The Button Family
By Beverly Blasucci

Make a button family, using different sized buttons for the faces. Only two-hole buttons can be used because the holes are the eyes.

Paint the face, or glue on features cut from felt or other material. Tiny sequins and beads can also be used. Add ears and eyeglasses to some of your characters.

Cover the back of the head with yarn hair. It can be braided, looped, or shredded.

Make a skeleton-type body, using colored or white pipe cleaners. Twist a loop where the head goes. Loop the ends of arms and legs for hands and feet.

Lay the pipe-cleaner figure on a piece of material. Make an outline for the clothes. Cut out, and sew to the body. Add bits of lace or rick-rack for decorations. Glue the button head in place.

Screen Weaving
By Lee Lindeman

An old or extra piece of window screen is wonderful to use for weaving a picture. Use yarn or string and a needle that will go through the holes in the screen easily.

Mount the finished weaving on colored poster board. For a different effect, tape the weaving on a window.

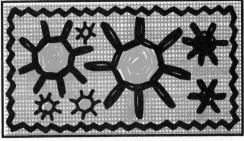

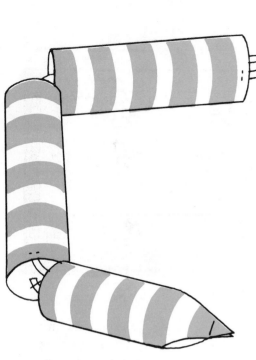

Wiggling Worm

By P. S. Zakroff

Wilbur, the Wiggling Worm, is made from three or more cardboard tubes, colored paper, rubber bands, paste, and staples.

Cut open a rubber band. Staple one end of it to the inside of one tube and the other end to the inside of a second tube. Do this again so that between every two tubes you have two bands. You can make Wilbur as long as you wish by adding more tubes and rubber bands.

On the end tube which is to be the head, mark and cut out a mouth. To make eyes, take a thin strip of colored paper about 4 inches long, loop the ends over, and paste them onto the top of the tube. Wilbur's bow tie is made just like the eyes, but pasted to the bottom of the tube behind the mouth. Two little squares of paper pasted to the upper tip of the mouth make a fine nose.

To make the tail, staple the end of the last tube closed. Using scissors, cut the end of the tube to a point. Give Wilbur stripes by cutting colored paper into thin strips and pasting them around the tubes.

Softy, the Saltbox Clown

By Kathryn Heisenfelt

This clown is made over a round cardboard saltbox. The costume is facial tissues used double as they pull from the box. Paint them with watercolors, or use colored tissues. The feet and the hand-arm pieces are cardboard. The facial features, hat, and ears are heavy construction paper. The ears are cut with tabs for inserting. The hat is a circle with a V cut out, then folded over to cone shape.

First paste on the feet and arms; then the baggy tissue pants about halfway up the box, folding, shaping, and pasting as you work. Lay the tissue for the shirt over the box, cut it to fit the arms, and paste in place.

The head is a small paper bag or piece of wrapping paper, stuffed lightly with cotton and tied at the neckline. Rip back a few strips at the tied end, stick the rest of the end through a hole punched in the box top, and paste the strips to the outside top. Shape the head and cover with white tissue. Paste on the facial features. Glue the ear tabs and run them through slits in the tissue. Paste in place the fringed-tissue hair, the hat, and a ruff around the neck. Make pompons from strips of tissue rolled loosely around a pencil, slipped off, and tied tightly. Paste these in place for the finishing touch.

Terry Dogs By Joy Warrell

Made of ordinary facecloths, these cute little dogs are inexpensive, simple, quick, and fun to do. They make nice party prizes and soft toys for babies, besides being an attractive decoration on a young girl's dresser.

Roll opposite sides of the facecloth toward the center until they meet. Keeping the rolled sides together, fold down the ends evenly (forming two corners) to make the legs. Tie cotton or string snugly around each corner to form the head and rear. With needle and thread tack the rolls together at the head, rear, and bottom of legs.

With colored thread, sew eyes, nose, and mouth on face. At the rear sew in several short strands of string to make the tail. Tie a ribbon around the neck.

Terry dogs can be made to stand, sit, or lie down.

Whirl-a-swirl

By Lee Lindeman

Cut a large circle from stiff cardboard. Plan a design for both sides of the circle, and paint on the designs with poster or tempera paint. Whirl your swirl into the sky. Look at the changes in your designs as it whirls.

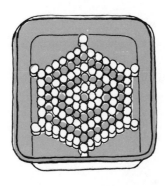

Crayon Pictures By Lee Lindeman

Tiny old bits of crayon that are too small to use for drawing can be used to make a very colorful picture. Draw and paint a very simple design on heavy cardboard, a thin piece of wood or Masonite, or inside a box cover. Slice the crayon bits into small pieces. Carefully glue crayon pieces of appropriate color to your designed board. Each piece should be glued very close to the next piece. Let it dry thoroughly.

Miniature Picture Case

By Katherine Corliss Bartow

Glue lace or braid around the front edges of a small aspirin box. Or cut flowers from a lace paper doily, and glue onto front and back of the box. Spray the box with gold paint inside and out.

The box may also be decorated with a decal or flower cutout after spraying.

Glue school photos or snapshots inside the box. These attractive picture cases can be carried in a purse, or stood upright on a bureau.

Five-dot Action Figures

By Lee Lindeman

Shut your eyes and make five dots on a piece of paper. Make sure that your dots are far apart. Using these dots as a guide, you can make stick figures of people running, jumping, falling, and in many other action positions.

Decide which dot will be the head. Draw a circle for the head and short lines for the neck and shoulders. Now decide which dots will become the feet. Draw hands around the last two dots. Connect the parts with lines. Don't forget the bending of knees and elbows.

The five-dot action figures are fun to draw at a party. With a friend making the dots, see if you can make a funny action figure.

Vegetable Puppets

By Vivian Smallowitz

Wouldn't it be fun to play with Hazel the Witch and her friends? They are all vegetable puppets, and they're very easy to make.

Witch Hazel. Select a short chunky carrot. Use an apple corer to carve a hole in the wide end, just large enough for your index finger. Attach the carved-out piece to the carrot with a straight pin to make a nose. Paint eyes and a mouth. Cut a circle of black construction paper and slip it over the pointed end to make a hat. Hazel's dress is a square of black cloth about the size of a man's handkerchief. Drape this over your hand and fasten with rubber bands around your thumb and middle finger. Fit the puppet over your cloth-covered index finger.

Oliver Owl. Cut a large potato in half and carve a hole in the cut end. Shape a slice of potato into a beak and attach with pins. Carve and paint the eyes and make feather ears. Oliver's body is a small paper bag, slit on one side for your hand and tied at the bottom with a rubber band.

Clarence the Clown. He is a white turnip with a radish nose and parsley hair. Cut the tip off a cone-shaped paper cup for his hat. A polka-dot kerchief and a paper doily ruffle make a nice clown suit.

Martin Martian. Pin a carrot-tip nose to a firm green pepper, and use nails or straight pins for the antennae. Paint eyes and a mouth. Make Martin's space suit out of a piece of aluminum foil draped over your hand. Form his feet with rubber bands tied around the corners.

You can make puppets out of other vegetables too. See the suggestions on this page; then use your imagination and design some of your own. One thing, though—they won't last forever, so play with them now!

Glass or Plastic Printing

By Lee Lindeman

Use a piece of flat glass with masking tape or adhesive tape around the edges, or a sheet of stiff plastic. With tempera paint, paint a scene or other design on the glass or plastic. While the paint is still wet, place a piece of paper over the wet paint on the glass. Gently pat and rub the paper with the palm of your hand. Carefully peel the paper print off the glass or plastic.

If you would like another print, refresh the design by putting more paint on the glass. Then repeat the printing process.

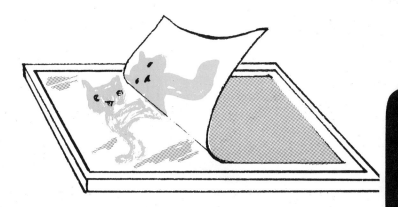

79

Snowball Faces

By Bess Lintner

The materials needed are medium-sized foam balls, common pins, crayons, sequins, and colored toothpicks. How would you like your snowball to feel—happy, sad, frightened? Use your imagination and add facial expressions to the foam balls, using the materials listed. Toothpicks inserted in the lower part of the ball form a support so that the head can stand.

Plaster of Paris Pendant

By Lee Lindeman

Mix ½ cup of water and a small amount of plaster of paris in a disposable container. The mixture should be as thick as melted ice cream. Using a spoon, put a small walnut-sized portion of moist plaster of paris on a piece of waxed paper. Make it into a pleasing shape. Carefully put a hole near the top as shown. Let the shape harden. Sandpaper until smooth.

Paint with tempera or poster paint. Give the pendant two coats of clear colorless nail polish for a shiny effect.

String the pendant on a chain, ribbon, cord, or string. It can be worn as an interesting and different piece of costume jewelry.

Plastic Bottle Mosaics

By Mildred K. Zibulka

Collect different-colored plastic detergent bottles. Cut them into ½-inch squares. They will look like mosaic tiles and can be put on paper plates, wood, or cardboard for beautiful effects.

Start with the center tile and work outward. If you are using a round paper plate, the edge tiles may be cut in half to fit. Leave about 1/16 of an inch between each tile so that the backing shows and becomes part of the design.

These tiles may also be used to make a picture. Keep it simple, tracing it lightly on the base. Use white glue to cement the tiles, putting a good-sized gob on the center back of each tile. Don't touch it again until it is thoroughly dry. The more colors you use, the more attractive the mosaic will be.

With masking tape attach a piece of yarn to the back of the plate for hanging. A pair of mosaics will make a very attractive wall decoration. Mosaics done on long rectangular pieces of plywood look especially well. These may be hung with tiny screw eyes and wire.

Easy-to-make Puppets

By Lee Lindeman

Wooden tongue depressors like those which your doctor uses can be made into puppets. Paint or draw a face at one end of the tongue depressor. Paste on paper or cloth details such as hair, ears, and feathers.

In the toe of an old sock make a slit just large enough for your finger and the tongue depressor. Glue the stick in place. On each side of the sock, near the toe, make a hole just large enough for your thumb and middle finger.

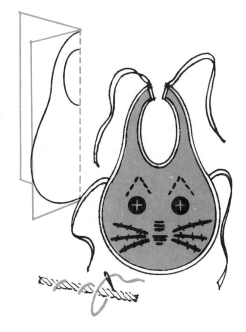

Kitten Apron

By Ella L. Langenberg

To make a pattern, hold a newspaper up against yourself to see how long you would like the apron, and how much you will need at the top to go around your neck. Then fold the paper in half lengthwise and draw the curved shape shown in the illustration. Cut out the pattern and try it on. If it doesn't fit, cut another. When you have a pattern that fits, pin it onto your material and cut out the cloth apron.

Sew on two black buttons for eyes, using white yarn or thread. Sew on eyebrows as shown with colored or black yarn, stitching in and out of the cloth. The small nose and mouth are sewn with red thread or yarn. Make one long stitch of black yarn for each whisker. With another thread sew over the yarn to hold it in place as illustrated.

Bind the edges with bias tape, using a contrasting color. Leave the ends of the tape long at the neck for a tie. Add a strip of tape at each side of the apron to tie around your waist.

Paper Playhouse

By Bernice P. Smith

Fold a 9-by-12-inch sheet of construction paper in half to 9-by-6. Cut off the corners at one 6-inch end to form a roof as shown. With pen or pencil, draw the roof tiles and a door at the bottom. On the front half of the house only, cut two sides of the door and fold it open on the third side. Draw windows with a line down the center, adding short lines on each side to form shutters. Cut open along the center line and across the top and bottom. Fold the shutters back.

From old magazines cut bright-colored pictures of tiny people. Paste them on the back half of the house so you can see them when the door or shutters are opened. Glue the playhouse together along the inside edges.

Print a street number over the door. Draw windowsills and a balcony. When the door is opened wide, the playhouse will stand up.

Creations From Old Greeting Cards

By E. M. Adduci

Look over your old greeting cards. Pick out the ones with objects which suggest a picture. Cut out the objects and paste them in place on plain paper. Use paints or crayons to finish the picture. You may wish to use glitter sprinkled onto glue as the final touch.

Bring the Birds Inside

By Alma C. Denny

Fill a small flowerpot with soil. Find a well-shaped branch, or several smaller branches. Push it far enough into the potted soil to hold it upright. Keep the soil moist and the branches will continue to remain fresh and green for quite a while.

Draw birds and color them on both sides with crayons so that they are vivid and alive-looking. Tie or staple them to the branches in natural positions.

This is a good decoration for a room at any time of the year, but is especially nice to have when there are few or no birds flying about outside.

81

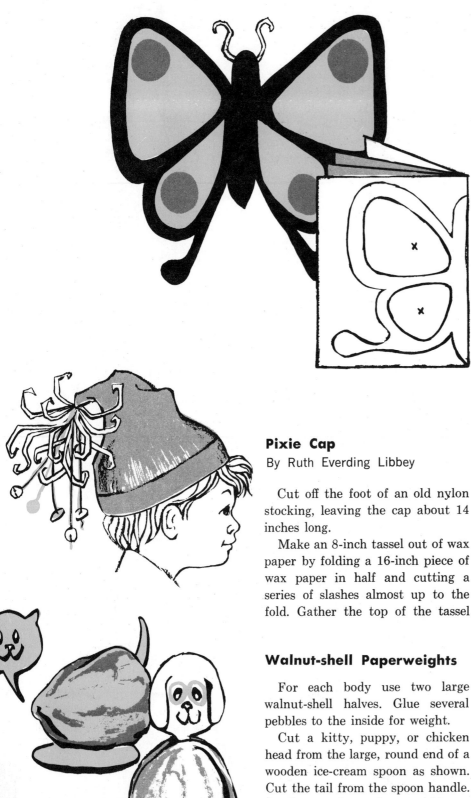

A Butterfly
By Joann M. Hart

Cut two rectangular pieces of black construction paper about 7 by 9 inches. Hold them together, and fold in half. Draw half a body and head on the folded edge, as shown in the small drawing. Then outline the wing parts, drawing a second outline about a half inch inside the first outline.

Cut out along the outside line. Pierce scissors through the X'd places and cut out these pieces.

Open the butterfly shapes and place them together with the pencil marks inside. Place colored tissue paper between the shapes and paste them together. Trim off excess. Paste on cut-out colored paper spots, staple on pipe-cleaner feelers, attach a thread, and hang in a window.

Pixie Cap
By Ruth Everding Libbey

Cut off the foot of an old nylon stocking, leaving the cap about 14 inches long.

Make an 8-inch tassel out of wax paper by folding a 16-inch piece of wax paper in half and cutting a series of slashes almost up to the fold. Gather the top of the tassel and tie with a piece of bright-colored yarn.

Insert the end of the tassle in the cut end of the stocking. Gather the stocking around it and tie with yarn. Add as many strands of yarn as you wish. Tie little bells or buttons here and there at the yarn ends. If desired, the cap may be filled with colored tissue. Use this cap for a costume party.

Walnut-shell Paperweights
By Texie Hering

For each body use two large walnut-shell halves. Glue several pebbles to the inside for weight.

Cut a kitty, puppy, or chicken head from the large, round end of a wooden ice-cream spoon as shown. Cut the tail from the spoon handle. Sandpaper the ends very thin to fit between the shell halves. Glue the two body parts together, inserting the glued head and tail at the proper place. Put rubber bands around the shell halves to hold them together till the glue is dry.

Cut the base from the large, round end of a wooden spoon and glue the body in place. Paint the body as desired. Draw on the features, ears, and paws as shown. Or you may prefer to cut the paws and ears from a spoon and insert them.

Paint the base a contrasting color.

Character Clips
By Katherine Corliss Bartow

These clips are handy for holding open books of all kinds or for keeping together mail, bills, or notes. They are made from spring-type clothespins.

A pair of clips decorated like the cook shown here would be nice for Mother when she is following a recipe. Draw the face in colors on pink paper. Glue it to the clothespin. Add yarn hair. Cut the clothes

and chef's hat from colored felt. Add tiny rickrack and lace trim. Color the shoes black. Glue a 2-inch piece of pipe cleaner between the prongs and bend to the front for arms. Cut a tiny spoon from a plastic food container lid and glue the hand around it.

Ink the Indian boy's features on the wood. Glue on black yarn hair, colored felt or corduroy headband and shirt, and brown paper pants.

See how many clip characters you can create.

Leaf Pictures
By Gladys Emerson

Collect leaves for your picture. Oak leaves are good for the girl. Fasten the leaves to a 9-by-12-inch piece of paper with gummed tape. With crayons draw the head, arms, and legs. A smaller leaf may be made into a dog or cat. Draw a leash from the little girl's hand to the animal's neck. After these pictures are completed, they should be pressed under something heavy for a day so that the leaves will dry without curling.

Candy Wrapper Picture
By Helen A. Thomas

Take a sheet of white paper and, with watercolors or a marking pen, draw a stem and leaves with a cloud-like base. If you use two shades of green for the leaves and stem, it will give depth to your picture.

For the flowers use cup-shaped candy wrappers which you twist, dip in glue, and place on the stems. For the flower centers glue scrap yarn or chenille pieces in the center. Mount the picture on bright-colored construction paper.

Gifts From Coffee Cans
By Lee Lindeman

A desk-top wastebasket, a cookie keeper, and a yarn or string holder —all of these useful articles can be made from a very large coffee can with a snap-on plastic cover.

From colored paper, cut or tear different and interesting shapes. Glue the shapes to completely cover the entire can. Be sure to decorate the can attractively and carefully.

If the can is to be a yarn or string holder, cut three holes in the plastic cover so you can pull the yarn or string through.

If it is a cookie keeper, do not put holes in the cover.

If it is a desk-top wastebasket, you don't even need the cover.

Year Round

Ballooney Animals By Vivian Smallowitz

Use long balloons in bright colors to create all kinds of gay ballooney animals. They make lovely table decorations and party favors.

On a large sheet of oaktag or lightweight cardboard, draw and cut out the head and front legs of an animal. Where the nose would be, cut out a 3-inch circle. Now draw the animal's back, including his hind legs and tail, and cut around them. Place the front half of the animal over the back half, lining up the feet. Trace inside the nose hole onto the back half, and cut out the circle to make matching holes in each half. With poster paints or watercolors, paint the animal to look natural, or make up your own color combinations.

Blow up a long balloon and knot the open end to keep it inflated. With the front and back pieces facing in the same direction, wedge opposite ends of the balloon through the holes in each half of the animal. Bend the legs slightly, if necessary, to make it stand.

Sweet Table Favors By Texie Hering

The owl shown is two large gumdrops fastened together with a piece of toothpick between, the body with the flat side down and the head with the flat side as the face. The eyes, ears, beak, feet, wings, and tail are cut from a colored soda straw and inserted into slits or holes made with a toothpick.

The lamb's head is a section of gumdrop, with soda-straw ears and tail, and bits of whole cloves for eyes, nose, and feet.

For place-card favors, dampen the bottom gumdrop and press it onto the card.

Use your imagination to make a different favor for each guest.

Plaster Leaf-print Plaques
By M. K. Towle

For the mold, use a plastic lid from a carton or can the size you want the finished plaque to be. Insert two heavy nails through the lid near the edge, about two inches apart. These will form the holes for hanging.

Gather some perfect leaves and select one no larger than your mold.

In a bowl mix plaster of paris, adding water a little at a time and stirring fast. It should be thin enough to pour, but not too runny.

Put the leaf face down in the lid with its tip centered between the two nails. Pour the plaster carefully on top of the leaf until the lid is full. Do not disturb it until the plaster sets. Clean your mixing bowl and spoon, as well as any plaster that may have spilled.

When you are sure the plaster is thoroughly set, carefully loosen the mold around the edges and gently remove the nails, and your plaque will come out. Peel away the leaf, and you have a perfect impression. Paint the leaf print or the background or both with water colors. Run a ribbon through the holes for hanging.

Write the name of the leaf on the back of the plaque. Why not start a collection and see how many different prints you can make?

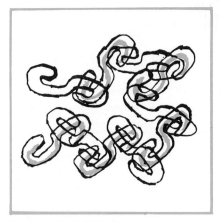

Paint-blot Flower
By Gladys Emerson

Fold a piece of white paper down the center, lengthwise. Open it. In the center fold near the top put a dab of tempera paint. Carefully close the fold and gently press the dab of paint out in all directions. If you do this carefully, you can form a very pretty flower. Cut leaves, stem, and flowerpot from colored construction paper, and paste them in place. It is fun to see how many different shapes of flowers you can make this way.

Paperclip Abstracts
By Helen A. Thomas

Open out paper clips and arrange them on a heavy sheet of white paper. With color marking pens, trace around the paper clips. Keep repeating and overlapping the design, and press harder in spots for an exciting picture. Leave open areas to give a sense of unity to your picture. Outline the sheet with a marking pen.

You can use this idea to make greeting cards, gift wrappings, or an edge or border.

Sawdust Sculpture
By S. M. Clotilde

Here is an easy and inexpensive way to learn sculpture. Pour 1/3 cup of water into an old plastic container. Slowly mix in wheat paste with a stick or old spoon until you have a creamy batter. Then add sawdust until the mixture is stiff enough for molding. A few drops of oil of cloves or peppermint will absorb the wheat paste odor.

Wearing rubber gloves, mold the figure you desire. A circle platform of sawdust beneath the figure will help keep it from losing form.

Let it dry for four or five days, turning it over occasionally so the underparts will dry. It will become as hard as wood, and can be sandpapered if a smooth surface is desired.

Decorate the figure with paint, ink, or oil crayon. When this is thoroughly dry, spray on a coat of shellac.

Toothpick Turkey Picture
By Lee Lindeman

On a black or dark-colored piece of paper, draw the outline of a turkey. Cover this outline with flat wooden toothpicks. Rub a small amount of clear-drying glue on a toothpick and place it over a section of the outline. To make shorter toothpick feathers, break the toothpicks into short pieces. To make a curved line on your picture, break the toothpick in several places, but not so that the toothpick is broken apart. Bend the toothpick and glue in place.

This method of making a picture can be used for many different designs. Try some ideas of your own.

Animal Friend Bookmarks
By Texie Hering

Make a paper pattern of a long-tailed animal. Use it to cut out the same shape from heavy construction paper. Paste this to the wrong side of a strip of fabric; then cut the fabric to the animal shape. Paste fabric to the other side and cut to shape. Add lines on both sides with ink to complete the animal. Bits of felt or other material could be used for features.

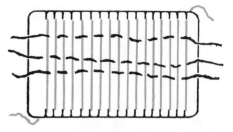

Things To Make

Woven Mat
By Lee Lindeman

You can make beautiful woven mats from the following easy-to-obtain materials: a rectangle of very stiff cardboard for the loom, strong thin string, yarn, scissors, and a comb.

On one long side of the cardboard draw a line ½ inch from the edge. Along this side, from the edge to the line, cut slits ½ inch apart to form tabs. Repeat this on the opposite long side. Tie string to one of the end tabs. String the loom by running the string back and forth over the front of the loom and under the tabs. Only one surface of the loom should have string on it; the other side should show only the loops around the tabs.

Cut lengths of yarn that are about 4 inches longer than the length of the loom. Weave the yarn in and out on the strings of the loom, leaving enough yarn at each end for a fringe. Use a comb to push back each length of yarn on the loom strings.

When you have finished weaving, carefully remove the mat by bending the cardboard tabs and carefully slipping off the strings. The two ends of the string will be loose and should be tied securely to the mat. Use sharp scissors to trim the fringe evenly.

Use any color combination that please you. The size of the mat will determine its use. A tiny one might even serve as a rug for a dollhouse.

A Storybook Tree
By Lawry Turpin

Do you like to read? Then you will need your own storybook tree. It will grow leaves or fruit every time you finish a story.

On heavy cardboard, draw the pattern as illustrated for the tree and stand. Cut out. Make slots in each piece as shown so that the tree will stand up. The slots should be as wide as the cardboard is thick. Paint the tree.

From colored paper, cut out leaves and fruit to be kept in an envelope. Each time you finish a storybook, write the name on a paper leaf or piece of fruit, and paste it on the tree. This will give you not only a complete record of all you read, but will encourage you to make your tree-of-knowledge grow.

Functional Bookmarks
By Doris P. Wilson

Functional bookmarks are so designed that they will really stay in place. In the elephant bookmark shown, the page top goes between the trunk and the tusks; in the sea horse, between the snout and the body.

When you make your own design, be sure it has the "clip-on" feature near the top, and an overall length of about 7 inches. The finished bookmark should be firm but not thick. Use felt backed with paper; or two thicknesses (and colors) of heavy construction paper or gummed crepe paper; or any other materials on hand. Add lines and other decoration with ink or paint or bits of paper.

If the bookmark is to be a gift, a hobby or other interest will suggest a very special design.

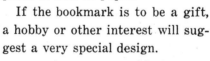

Gumdrop Flowers for Cookies

By Ursula Kannry

To make pretty decorations for cookies, you will need soft gumdrops of different colors, granulated sugar, and a rolling pin and breadboard. Sprinkle sugar onto the board. Cut a gumdrop in half and place half on the board. Roll this into a 2½-inch-long strip, turning the gumdrop after each stroke so that it will not stick.

Roll the strip with your fingers, pinching one side of it to form a stem. This will cause the other side to spread out like the petals of a blossom. Try two half-strips of different colors for a two-toned flower. Press onto a flat cooky.

Green gumdrops can be cut and pressed onto the cooky for leaves.

Crayon Resist

By Lee Lindeman

Draw a scene or a design on a large piece of paper. Press hard with your crayons to get the colors bright and waxy. After you have finished, brush over the whole drawing with a thin coat of watercolor paint. Use a large brush. It's fun to discover that the crayon shows through the paint almost like magic.

Texture Pictures

By Marilyn Burch

Gather objects which possess different textures, such as small stones, a piece of sponge, burlap, paper grass, sand, bark, or colored paper. Choose a lid from a cardboard box. The picture will be made inside this lid.

Design a picture which contains textures of things you have collected. With the above material you might make a seashore scene. The water and sky might be blue tissue paper; the beach, sand and pebbles pasted in place; the treetop, a sponge; and a cabin, a piece of bark. When the picture is completed, stretch clear cellophane over the top of the lid. Use your imagination and make your own collection of texture pictures.

Viking Troll

By Katherine Corliss Bartow

Cut two cups from an egg carton. Glue open ends together. Paint the lower cup brown. To the upper cup glue paper eyes with blue centers, and a 3/8-inch-long nose cut from the end of one of the high, narrow peak dividers. Paint the nose and cheeks pink. Add yarn strands for hair and moustache.

For the helmet, punch two holes in a cardboard circle. Insert round toothpick pieces at an angle and glue in place. Paint the helmet gold. Glue it to the head.

Punch holes and glue in pipe cleaner arms. Add a toothpick staff. Cut feet from heavy black paper and glue them in place.

87

Fan Easter Card   By Katherine Corliss Bartow

Cut an 8-inch circle from heavy drawing paper. Fold it in half. Fold this half into three equal sections with section A on top.

Cut ten 1¼-inch Easter eggs from gift wrapping paper. Glue two eggs each on the front of A and B. Open·card to a circle and glue six eggs spaced evenly around the curved edge. Outline each egg with glitter.

Refold the card and print on the front of B, WISHING YOU. On A print A HAPPY. Open the card and print EASTER, one letter under each of the six eggs. Glue a pink paper rabbit and cutouts from lace paper doilies inside.

Punch a hole through section A at the bottom. Double a 14-inch length of silk cord or yarn. Pass the center loop through the hole from the front. Pass the cord ends through the loop. Knot and fringe the ends.

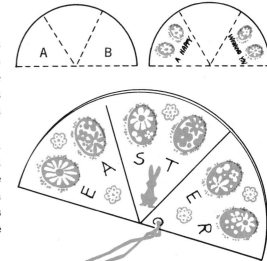

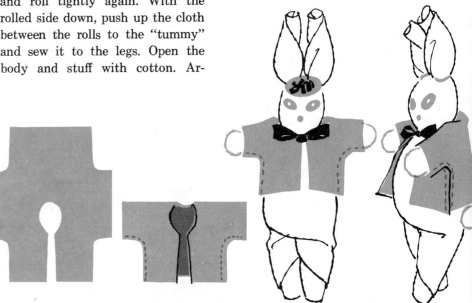

3-D Rabbits and Chicks
By Lee Lindeman

Use a cardboard ring from a roll of masking tape or ribbon, or make your own cardboard ring.

On the side of the ring, glue the shape of a rabbit cut from heavy paper. Glue an identical rabbit to the other side of the ring.

The ear centers, eyes, nose, and other details can be cut from paper or felt, and glued to the rabbit. Or these details can be added with crayons or paint.

A 3-D chick can be made in a similar way.

Washcloth Bunnies   By Kathryn Heisenfelt

Roll in two sides of the washcloth tightly till they meet at the center. Pin at the middle with a safety pin.

To make the ears, hold the cloth with the rolled sides down. Push cloth down between the rolls halfway to the pin. Tie each ear at the base with heavy pink thread. Then tie the cloth firmly at the middle to form the head, and remove the pin. Open out the head, stuff with cotton, and sew shut. For legs, open the rolled ends slightly, tuck a thin layer of cotton up into each side, and roll tightly again. With the rolled side down, push up the cloth between the rolls to the "tummy" and sew it to the legs. Open the body and stuff with cotton. Arrange the bunny to sit up, then sew up the back.

Cut the coat from felt and sew up the sides. Stuff cotton-ball hands in the sleeves and sew in place. Place the coat around the body. Attach a thread from one shoulder to the other to hold it in place. Sew a flattened cotton ball in place for the tail.

Paste on pink felt eyes and mouth, and felt hat. Tie a colored bow around the neck, and paste a small one on the hat.

A Picture With Three-Dimensional Flower Blossoms

By Lee Lindeman

A picture of daisies, daffodils, dandelions, and many other kinds of flowers can be created from parts of an egg carton. Ask your mother to save molded-type egg cartons.

Cut out a few of the cup shapes from the carton. Cut and trim each cup so that it has a scalloped edge. When painted with poster or tempera paint, the cups become the flower blossoms. Place, but do not glue, the egg-carton blossoms on a stiff piece of paper or cardboard. Plan and paint a pleasing arrangement of flowers on the heavy piece of paper or cardboard. After your painting is dry, glue the egg-carton flowers on the right places.

Your beautiful flower picture is now ready for you to frame.

Strike, Scrape, and Shake

Make a Family of Percussion Instruments

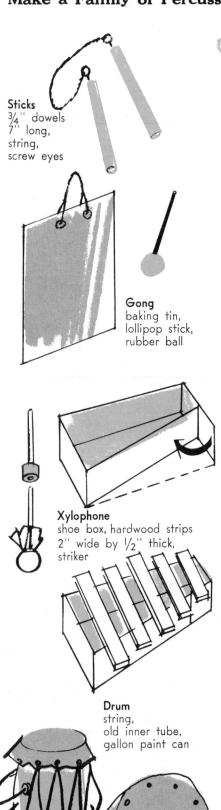

Sticks
3/4" dowels
7" long,
string,
screw eyes

Gong
baking tin,
lollipop stick,
rubber ball

Xylophone
shoe box, hardwood strips
2" wide by 1/2" thick,
striker

Drum
string,
old inner tube,
gallon paint can

Percussion instruments are sounded in one of three ways: striking, scraping, or shaking.

Among the **strikers** are drums, cymbals, chimes, the gong, xylophone, triangle, wood blocks, and rhythmic sticks. The **scrapers** include sandpaper blocks which are rubbed together, and notched gourds which are rubbed with a thin stick. The **shakers** have loose parts which rattle or jingle, such as the pellet-filled gourds called maracas, and the tambourine with loose metal discs around the rim.

You can easily make some simple percussion instruments from each group. Materials needed are listed with the drawings. Additional instructions are given below.

Sticks. The string is simply to keep the sticks as a set.

Gong. Lay tin on a board and hammer out holes with large nail.

Xylophone. Experiment with various lengths. The shorter the key, the higher the pitch.

Drum. Remove bottom of can with can opener. Turn down rough edges with pliers. Lace rubber circles together as tightly as possible.

Scraper. Notch a 1-foot dowel. Rub smaller stick along notches.

Sand Blocks. Buy artist's sandpaper pads, or glue sandpaper to flat sticks. Rub them together.

Wrist Bells. Sew sleigh bells to band. Make one for each wrist.

Jingle. Use various sizes of buttons to rattle together loosely.

Maracas. Experiment with rice, tapioca, corn, or dried beans for filler, before stapling pie pans. Make one for each hand.

Scraper
two dowel sticks

Sand Blocks
sandpaper and
flat sticks; or buy
artists' sandpaper pads

Wrist Bells
sleigh bells, elastic band

Jingle
clothespin,
flatheaded nail,
buttons

Maracas
aluminum foil pans,
Popsicle sticks,
staples, filler

Characters and Creatures

By Lee Lindeman

Is it a goblin, a robin, a bee, or a knight? All of these can be created from the cardboard tube from a roll of toilet tissue. Gather up some of these tubes and have some fun.

You will need to form a point at one end of the tube for the head of the creature. Draw a line around the tube about 1½ inches from the end. Then cut about six 1½-inch slits from the end of the tube to the line. The slits should be evenly spaced around the tube. Cut a point on each piece of cardboard between the slits. Push these points together and glue to form the point. The tube is now closed at one end. This is the head of your character.

Will your creature be a bird, an angel, a fish, or a person? Use thin cardboard or construction paper for arms and feet, wings, tails, beaks, or ears. Toothpicks and pipe cleaners make wonderful legs for bugs and birds. Use wire, pipe cleaners, and cotton swabs for whiskers and feelers. An old spring or a curled-up pipe cleaner might be used for a curly tail.

Paint your character or creature with poster paint. Let each color dry before you put on the next color. Use a small brush for painting the details. Let your imagination run wild.

91

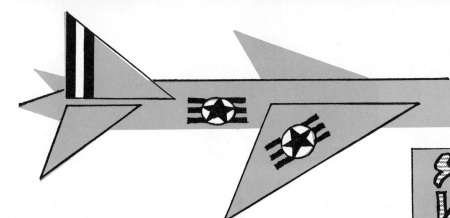

Winter Diorama

By Joann M. Hart

Draw a winter landscape on a 9-by-12-inch sheet of white construction paper, using colored chalk, crayons, or water paints. Use the 9-inch edges as the sides of your picture.

On a 6-by-9-inch piece of black construction paper, mark off a 1-inch border. Above the bottom border draw with white chalk a mound of snow and a snowman. Mark off a lamppost beside the snowman. With colored chalk make the face, buttons, hat, and lamp. Then cut out along the inside frame line, snow mound, snowman, and lamp. Fold each side of the landscape forward one inch. Apply paste along these folds and attach the cutout.

Jet Plane

By Millie H. Emerson

Glue a cone-shaped paper cup over each end of a cardboard tube such as wax paper comes on. Cut triangles from cardboard for fins and tail section. Insert them in slits cut in the body section. Paint the finished product and add insignia for a very modern-looking jet plane.

Mama and Papa Spool

By Sandra E. Csippan

Glue together two large spools and one small one for Papa. And one large and two small spools for Mama. After the glue is thoroughly dry, paint the spools as desired. Add facial features. For arms, wrap a pipe cleaner around the spool just under the head.

Cut a lace-paper doily to shape for Mama's hat. Add a pompon or bead on the top. Use a toothpaste-tube top for Papa's hat.

Corrugated Cardboard Creations

By Lee Lindeman

From the smooth straight side of a corrugated cardboard box, cut a square or rectangular piece large enough for a picture.

Make a drawing on the smooth piece of corrugated cardboard with a dry marker, dark crayon, or ink. Using a single-edged razor blade or the tip of a mat knife, cut along the inside of some of the outlined areas of your picture. Cut only through the top layer of cardboard and peel it off, thus revealing the ripply inner layer of cardboard. Carefully pick off the tiny pieces that may have stuck to the inner layer.

Paint the plain, smooth areas that are left with tempera or poster paint.

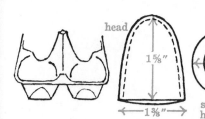

Egg-carton Finger Puppets

By Katherine Corliss Bartow

Use the kind of egg carton that has the tall, pointed dividers down the center of the two rows of cups. Cut out these finger-shaped dividers for your puppet bodies. It will be fun to create characters from your favorite stories, and the little puppets also make a decorative miniature collection.

Some ideas are suggested here to start with. The heads, except for the snow people, are light-colored cloth. Cut two pieces like the pattern shown, and sew together except at the bottom. Turn inside out and stuff half full with cotton. Dab glue on the top third of the puppet body. Fit the head down over it and press it to the glue. Tie a thread around the neck. Features and buttons are paper, felt, or colored crayon. Hands, paws, mittens, and ears are felt.

Dresses are felt or heavy cloth.

The cat has pink head and paws; blue eyes, ears, and body; and a red ribbon bow.

The lion has a yellow head and paws, brown body and ears, and light-brown yarn for the mane.

Leave more width on the bottom when cutting the dividers for the snow people. Paint them white. Add features and red yarn scarfs. The snowman's hat is a cardboard circle, cut like pattern shown. Paint it black and place down over the head. Paint the top of the head black for the crown.

Cardboard Tube Friend

By Sandra E. Csippan

Cut one end of a cardboard tube into points. Cut a slit on each side of the tube, and insert a Popsicle stick. Then paint the tube. After it is dry, paint a face or draw one with a felt pen. Make a skirt from the sides of a fluted paper baking cup, and glue to the tube.

Stick Doll

By Lois Hoadley Dick

Paste five Popsicle sticks together as shown, for the body. Add a circle head of heavy pink paper. Paste on braided yarn hair, and buttons for eyes and mouth. For a boy doll, add a felt hat in place of the braid.

Pop-it Puppet Heads By Lee Lindeman

You can make wonderful "pop it on your finger" puppet heads from fruit separators. Ask your grocer to save the separators for you. Cut out two of the round cuplike sections. Fit the edges together. If they do not fit, one of the pieces may need trimming. Glue the two pieces together carefully and let dry. Carefully cut a hole at the bottom of this head large enough for one or two fingers to fit into.

Paint the puppet head with tempera paint. Use a small brush

to paint on the small details. Hair can be made from cloth, yarn, old fur, or cotton. Glue it on carefully.

Make a puppet head for each hand and produce your own puppet show.

Window Shade Pulls

By Texie Hering

From green felt cut four leaves and one stem. From contrasting colored felt cut two flower shapes like the pattern, with a hole in the center as shown. Cut a circle of corrugated paper with a hole in the center to go between these flower shapes.

Push a colored glass marble into the hole of the paper circle. Loop a 16-inch length of colored string and knot the ends together. Paste the knotted end of the loop around the marble. Add the tips of the leaves and stem to the circle as shown. Then paste on the flower shapes, one on each side of the circle. Outline the petal shapes of the flowers with white ink or paint.

Attach to the window shade in place of your present pull, and see how prettily the light shines through the marble.

Cardboard Roll People

By Sandra Csippan

The boy and girl shown were drawn in pencil on a length of cardboard tubing, then tempera-painted in appropriate colors. The hats are paper nut cups painted with tempera.

Change the drawings and trim to create your own people.

By pasting a cardboard circle at the bottom, the tube becomes a container for which you can find many uses.

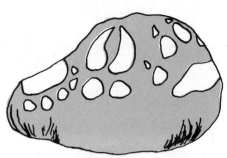

Animal Tracks Paperweight

By June Rose Mobly

Choose a smooth rock and paint it a bright color. When the paint is dry, glue a small piece of felt to the bottom. Turn the rock over, and on the top side, draw lightly with pencil the tracks of several different kinds of animals. Paint these white. When the white paint is dry, outline each footprint with a different color felt-point pen.

Spring Candy Flowers

By James W. Perrin, Jr.

Brightly colored jelly beans make excellent flowers. Glue the candy with white glue and add pipe cleaners for stems and leaves. Be sure to have some extra candy for nibbling. Sometimes the material for this project disappears in mysterious ways and can never be found again!

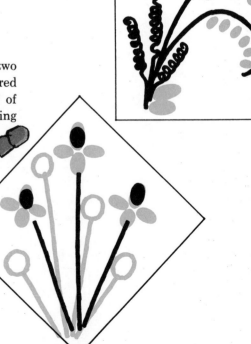

Delectable Dachshunds By Aline Ray

These "dogs" make unusual party favors, and they can be eaten, too.

Use a firm banana for the body. Run small gumdrops onto seven toothpicks and insert them into the body for the four legs, the two ears, and the tail. Add a single red gumdrop for a tongue, and half of a black one for each eye, fastening them with pieces of toothpick.

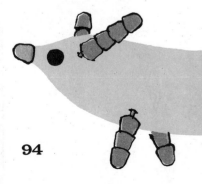

Hand-outline Creations

By Lee Lindeman

You can create all kinds of pictures, using the outline of your hand as a basic design—animals, trees, Indians, imaginary birds and animals, and even abstract art. Use crayon, chalk, dry markers, or pencil for your hand drawings.

Draw around your hand while holding your fingers spread apart. Now turn the paper in various positions—upside down and sideways. What does this shape suggest to you? You might make a giraffe by adding a long neck and a head. If you draw a face on the palm of the outline, the fingers will become feathers for an Indian. From other drawings of your hand, you might create horses, hula dancers, or birds. Just use your imagination.

Now hold your hand with the fingers together, and draw the outline. What does this new shape suggest? When you have thought of all the possibilities for this shape, try it with your thumb held apart from the other fingers. There are several other hand positions you may also try.

The illustrations show a number of creations. How many more can you make?

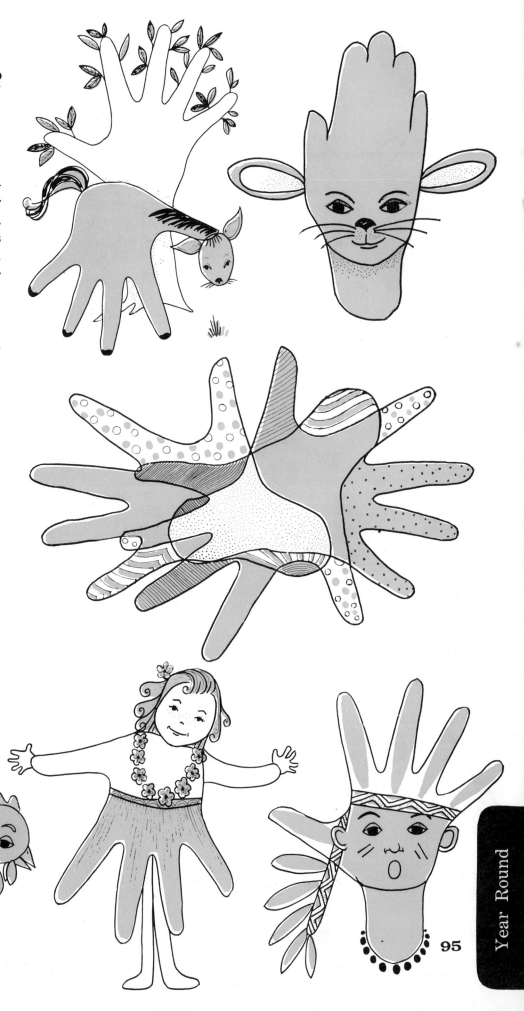

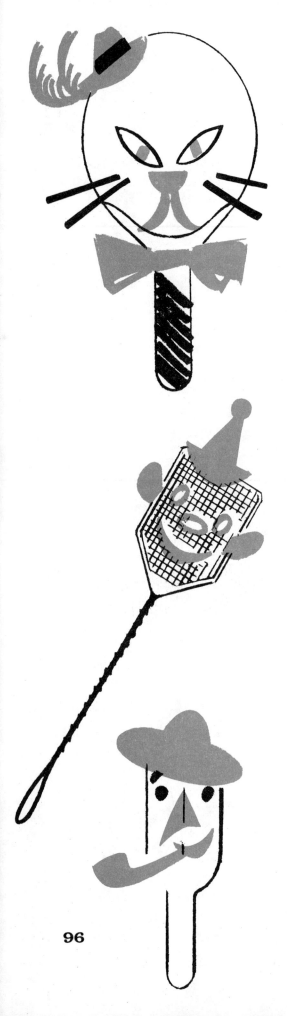

Puppets

By Nelly Allan

Puppets are fascinating to create and put into action. They can be made from many different objects, a few of which are suggested here. The illustrations are intended only as examples. Use your imagination to create your own characters from whatever materials you have on hand.

The fly swatter, Ping-Pong paddle, and sugar scoop each have a ready-made handle.

The wooden clothespin can be covered, and manipulated from underneath.

The plastic bottle needs a spatula or flat wooden stick fastened to the bottle for a handle before decorating the bottle.

Paper bags are decorated on one side only, and are manipulated with your hand inside the bag.

For the balloon puppet, blow up a small, round balloon. Cover it with strips of gauze dipped in wet plaster of paris or glue, crisscrossing them until the balloon is entirely covered. Pinch the wet gauze into nose, mouth, and eye shapes. When entirely dry, puncture the head with a pin to let out the air. Glue the head to a piece of cardboard tubing for the neck. Add clothing. Manipulate the puppet from underneath with a finger through each sleeve.